Introducing ZFS on Linux

Understand the Basics of Storage with ZFS

Damian Wojsław

Apress®

Introducing ZFS on Linux: Understand the Basics of Storage with ZFS

Damian Wojsław
ul. Duńska 27i/8, Szczecin, 71-795 Zachodniopomorskie, Poland

ISBN-13 (pbk): 978-1-4842-3305-4   ISBN-13 (electronic): 978-1-4842-3306-1
https://doi.org/10.1007/978-1-4842-3306-1

Library of Congress Control Number: 2017960448

Managing Director: Welmoed Spahr
Editorial Director: Todd Green
Acquisitions Editor: Louise Corrigan
Development Editor: James Markham
Technical Reviewer: Sander van Vugt
Coordinating Editor: Nancy Chen
Copy Editor: Kezia Endsley
Compositor: SPi Global
Indexer: SPi Global
Artist: SPi Global

Distributed to the book trade worldwide by Springer Science+Business Media New York, 233 Spring Street, 6th Floor, New York, NY 10013. Phone 1-800-SPRINGER, fax (201) 348-4505, e-mail orders-ny@springer-sbm.com, or visit www.springeronline.com. Apress Media, LLC is a California LLC and the sole member (owner) is Springer Science + Business Media Finance Inc (SSBM Finance Inc). SSBM Finance Inc is a **Delaware** corporation.

For information on translations, please e-mail rights@apress.com, or visit http://www.apress.com/rights-permissions.

Apress titles may be purchased in bulk for academic, corporate, or promotional use. eBook versions and licenses are also available for most titles. For more information, reference our Print and eBook Bulk Sales web page at http://www.apress.com/bulk-sales.

Any source code or other supplementary material referenced by the author in this book is available to readers on GitHub via the book's product page, located at www.apress.com/9781484233054. For more detailed information, please visit http://www.apress.com/source-code.

Printed on acid-free paper

To my Wife Ada and my Kids - Iga and Mikołaj

Table of Contents

About the Author

Damian Wojsław, a long-time illumos and ZFS enthusiast, has worked with ZFS storage from a few hundred gigabytes up to hundreds of terabytes capacity. For several years, he was a Field Engineer at Nexenta Systems, Inc., a Software Defined Storage company, and he installed and supported a large number of the company's customers. He has been an active member of OpenSolaris and later on illumos communities, with special interest in ZFS, and later OpenZFS. He started working professionally with Linux in 1999 and since then uses Linux and Unix exclusively on his servers and desktops.

His professional curriculum vitae is hosted on his LinkedIn profile.[1]

---

[1]https://pl.linkedin.com/in/damian-wojsław-559722a0

About the Technical Reviewer

Sander van Vugt is an independent trainer and consultant living in the Netherlands and working throughout the European Union. He specializes in Linux and Novell systems, and he has worked with both for more than 10 years. Besides being a trainer, he is also an author, having written more than 20 books and hundreds of technical articles. He is a Master Certified Novell Instructor (MCNI) and holds LPIC-1 and -2 certificates, as well as all important Novell certificates.

Acknowledgments

The book wouldn't be possible without endless crowd of people that taught me how to learn, how to look for answers and about ZFS. In particular I would like to thank Lech Karol Pawłaszek for showing me how to be transparent and kind to customers, Darryl Clark, Pete Turner, Michael Green, Daniel Borek, Michał Bielicki and all other Nexenta people for helping me while I struggled, Darek Ankowski for introducing me to ZFS, Leszek Krupiński and all of old apcoh - you all know what for. Greatest thanks to Louise Corrigan and all Apress editorial staff for making me finish this book.

Introduction

Why Linux?

I started my Linux journey in 1997, when my brother and I got our hands on a Slackware CD. We were thrilled and, at the same time, mystified. It was our first contact with a Unix-like operating system. The only command-line we knew at that point was DOS. Everything—from commands to mountpoints to paths—was different and mysterious. Back then, it was really a hobbyist OS. Now Linux is a major player in the server land. Almost everything out there, on the Internet, runs on Linux. Web servers, mail servers, cloud solutions, you name it—you can be almost sure Linux is underneath.

Its popularity makes Linux the perfect platform for learning ZFS. I assume that most of my readers are Linux admins, thus I will deal only with ZFS itself as a novelty.

CHAPTER 1

ZFS Overview

To work with ZFS, it's important to understand the basics of the technical side and implementation. I have seen lots of failures that have stemmed from the fact that people were trying to administer or even troubleshoot ZFS file systems without really understanding what they were doing and why. ZFS goes to great lengths to protect your data, but nothing in the world is user proof. If you try really hard, you will break it. That's why it's a good idea to get started with the basics.

Note   On most Linux distributions, ZFS is not available by default. For up-to-date information about the implementation of ZFS on Linux, including the current state and roadmap, visit the project's home page: `http://zfsonlinux.org/`. Since Ubuntu Xenial Xerus, the 16.04 LTS Ubuntu release, Canonical has made ZFS a regular, supported file system. While you can't yet use it during the installation phase, at least not easily, it is readily available for use and is a default file system for LXD (a next-generation system container manager).

In this chapter, we look at what ZFS is and cover some of the key terminology.

© Damian Wojsław 2017
D. Wojsław, *Introducing ZFS on Linux*, https://doi.org/10.1007/978-1-4842-3306-1_1

What Is ZFS?

ZFS is a copy-on-write (COW) file system that merges a file system, logical volume manager, and software RAID. Working with a COW file system means that, with each change to the block of data, the data is written to a completely new location on the disk. Either the write occurs entirely, or it is not recorded as done. This helps to keep your file system clean and undamaged in the case of a power failure. Merging the logical volume manager and file system together with software RAID means that you can easily create a storage volume that has your desired settings and contains a ready-to-use file system.

Note   ZFS's great features are no replacement for backups. Snapshots, clones, mirroring, etc., will only protect your data as long as enough of the storage is available. Even having those nifty abilities at your command, you should still do backups and test them regularly.

COW Principles Explained

The Copy On Write (COW) design warrants a quick explanation, as it is a core concept that enables some essential ZFS features. Figure 1-1 shows a graphical representation of a possible pool; four disks comprise two vdevs (two disks in each vdev). vdev is a virtual device built on top of disks, partitions, files or LUNs. Within the pool, on top of vdevs, is a file system. Data is automatically balanced across all vdevs, across all disks.

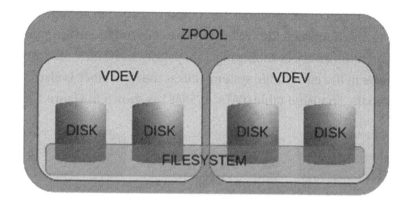

Figure 1-1. *Graphical representation of a possible pool*

Figure 1-2 presents a single block of freshly written data.

Figure 1-2. *Single data block*

When the block is later modified, it is not being rewritten. Instead, ZFS writes it anew in a new place on disk, as shown in Figure 1-3. The old block is still on the disk, but ready for reuse, if free space is needed.

Figure 1-3. *Rewritten data block*

Let's assume that before the data has been modified, the system operator creates a snapshot. The DATA 1 SNAP block is being marked as belonging to the file system snapshot. When the data is modified and

3

written in new place, the old block location is recorded in a snapshot vnodes table. Whenever a file system needs to be restored to the snapshot time (when rolling back or mounting a snapshot), the data is reconstructed from vnodes in the current file system, unless the data block is also recorded in the snapshot table (DATA 1 SNAP) as shown in Figure 1-4.

Figure 1-4. Snapshotted data block

Deduplication is an entirely separate scenario. The blocks of data are being compared to what's already present in the file system and if duplicates are found, only a new entry is added to the deduplication table. The actual data is not written to the pool. See Figure 1-5.

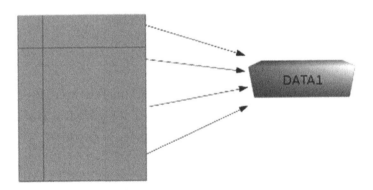

Figure 1-5. Deduplicated data block

ZFS Advantages

There are many storage solutions out in the wild for both large enterprises and SoHo environments. It is outside the scope of this guide to cover them in detail, but we can look at the main pros and cons of ZFS.

Simplified Administration

Thanks to merging volume management, RAID, and file system all in one, there are only two commands you need use to create volumes, redundancy levels, file systems, compression, mountpoints, etc. It also simplifies monitoring, since there are two or even three less layers to be looked out for.

Proven Stability

ZFS has been publicly released since 2005 and countless storage solutions have been deployed based on it. I've seen hundreds of large ZFS storages in big enterprises and I'm confident the number is hundreds if not thousands more. I've also seen small, SoHo ZFS arrays. Both worlds have witnessed great stability and scalability, thanks to ZFS.

Data Integrity

ZFS was designed with data integrity in mind. It comes with data integrity checks, metadata checksumming, data failure detection (and, in the case of redundant setup, possibly fixing it), and automatic replacement of failed devices.

Scalability

ZFS scales well, with the ability to add new devices, control cache, and more.

ZFS Limitations

As with every file system, ZFS also has its share of weaker points that you need to keep in mind to successfully operate the storage.

80% or More Principle

As with most file systems, ZFS suffers terrible performance penalty when filled up to 80% or more of its capacity. It is a common problem with file systems. Remember, when your pool starts filling to 80% of capacity, you need to look at either expanding the pool or migrating to a bigger setup.

You cannot shrink the pool, so you cannot remove drives or vdevs from it once they have been added.

Limited Redundancy Type Changes

Except for turning a single disk pool into a mirrored pool, you cannot change redundancy type. Once you decide on a redundancy type, your only way of changing it is to destroy the pool and create a new one, recovering data from backups or another location.

Key Terminology

Some key terms that you'll encounter are listed in the following sections.

Storage Pool

The *storage pool* is a combined capacity of disk drives. A pool can have one or more file systems. File systems created within the pool see all the pool's capacity and can grow up to the available space for the whole pool. Any one file system can take all the available space, making it impossible for other file systems in the same pool to grow and contain new data. One of the ways to deal with this is to use space reservations and quotas.

vdev

vdev is a virtual device that can consist of one or more physical drives. vdev can be a pool or be a part of a larger pool. vdev can have a redundancy level of mirror, triple mirror, RAIDZ, RAIDZ-2, or RAIDZ-3. Even higher levels of mirror redundancy are possible, but are impractical and costly.

File System

A *file system* is created in the boundaries of a pool. A ZFS file system can only belong to one pool, but a pool can contain more than one ZFS file system. ZFS file systems can have reservations (minimum guaranteed capacity), quotas, compression, and many other properties. File systems can be nested, meaning you can create one file system in another. Unless you specify otherwise, file systems will be automatically mounted within their parent. The uppermost ZFS file system is named the same as the pool and automatically mounted under the root directory, unless specified otherwise.

Snapshots

Snapshots are point-in-time snaps of the file system's state. Thanks to COW semantics, they are extremely cheap in terms of disk space. Creating a snapshot means recording file system vnodes and keeping track of them. Once the data on that inode is updated (written to new place—remember, it is COW), the old block of data is retained. You can access the old data view by using said snapshot, and only use as much space as has been changed between the snapshot time and the current time.

7

Clones

Snapshots are read-only. If you want to mount a snapshot and make changes to it, you'll need a read-write snapshot, or *clone*. Clones have many uses, one of greatest being boot environment clones. With an operating system capable of booting off ZFS (illumos distributions, FreeBSD), you can create a clone of your operating system and then run operations in a current file system or in a clone, to perhaps upgrade the system or install a tricky video driver. You can boot back to your original working environment if you need to, and it only takes as much disk space as the changes that were introduced.

Dataset

A *dataset* is a ZFS pool, file system, snapshot, volume, and clone. It is the layer of ZFS where data can be stored and retrieved.

Volume

A *volume* is a file system that emulates the block device. It cannot be used as a typical ZFS file system. For all intents and purposes, it behaves like a disk device. One of its uses is to export it through iSCSI or FCoE protocols, to be mounted as LUNs on a remote server and then used as disks.

Note   Personally, volumes are my least favorite use of ZFS. Many of the features I like most about ZFS have limited or no use for volumes. If you use volumes and snapshot them, you cannot easily mount them locally for file retrieval, as you would when using a simple ZFS file system.

Resilvering

Resilvering is the process of rebuilding redundant groups after disk replacement. There are many reasons you may want to replace a disk—perhaps the drive becomes faulted, or you decide to swap the disk for any other reason—once the new drive is added to the pool, ZFS will start to restore data to it. This is a very obvious advantage of ZFS over traditional RAIDs. Only data is being resilvered, not whole disks.

Note   Resilvering is a low-priority operating system process. On a very busy storage system, it will take more time.

Pool Layout Explained

Pool Layout is the way that disks are grouped into vdevs and vdevs are grouped together into the ZFS pool.

Assume that we have a pool consisting of six disks, all of them in RAIDZ-2 configuration (rough equivalent of RAID-6). Four disks contain data and two contain parity data. Resiliency of the pool allows for losing up to two disks. Any number above that will irreversibly destroy the file system and result in the need for backups.

Figure 1-6 presents the pool. While it is technically possible to create a new vdev of fewer or larger number of disks, with different sizes, it will almost surely result in performance issues.

Figure 1-6. *Single vdev RAIDZ-2 pool*

And remember—you cannot remove disks from a pool once the vdevs are added. If you suddenly add a new vdev, say, four disks RAIDZ, as in Figure 1-7, you compromise pool integrity by introducing a vdev with lower resiliency. You will also introduce performance issues.

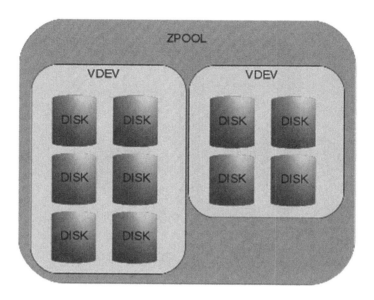

Figure 1-7. Wrongly enhanced pool

The one exception of "cannot change the redundancy level" rule is single disk to mirrored and mirrored to even more mirrored. You can attach a disk to a single disk vdev, and that will result in a mirrored vdev (see Figure 1-8). You can also attach a disk to a two-way mirror, creating a triple-mirror (see Figure 1-9).

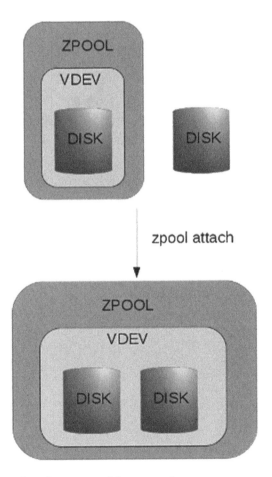

Figure 1-8. Single vdev turned into a mirror

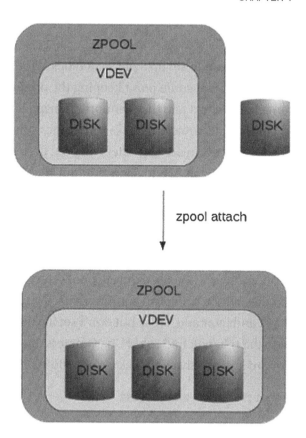

Figure 1-9. *Two way mirror into a three-way mirror*

Common Tuning Options

A lot of tutorials tell you to set two options (one pool level and one file system level) that are supposed to increase the speed. Unfortunately, most of them don't explain what they do and why they should work: `ashift=12` and `atime=off`.

While the truth is, they may offer a significant performance increase, setting them blindly is a major error. As stated previously, to properly administer your storage server, you need to understand why you use options that are offered.

ashift

The ashift option allows you to set up a physical block layout on disks. As disk capacities kept growing, at some point keeping the original block size of 512 bytes became impractical and disk vendors changed it to 4096 bytes. But for backward compatibility reasons, disks sometimes still advertise 512 block sizes. This can have an adverse effect on pool performance. The ashift option was introduced in ZFS to allow manual change of block sizing done by ZFS. Since it's specified as a binary shift, the value is a power, thus: $2^\wedge12 = 4096$. Omitting the ashift option allows ZFS to detect the value (the disk can lie about it); using value of 9 will set the block size to 512. The new disk block size is called Advanced Layout (AL).

The ashift option can only be used during pool setup or when adding a new device to a vdev. Which brings up another issue: if you create a pool by setting up ashift and later add a disk but don't set it, your performance may go awry due to the mismatched ashift parameters. If you know you used the option or are unsure, always check before adding new devices:

```
trochej@madchamber:~$ sudo zpool list
```

```
NAME SIZE  ALLOC FREE  EXPANDSZ FRAG CAP DEDUP HEALTH ALTROOT
data 2,72T 133G  2,59T -         3%   4% 1.00x ONLINE -
trochej@madchamber:~$ sudo zpool get all data
```

NAME	PROPERTY	VALUE	SOURCE
data	size	2,72T	-
data	capacity	4%	-
data	altroot	-	default
data	health	ONLINE	-
data	guid	7057182016879104894	default
data	version	-	default
data	bootfs	-	default
data	delegation	on	default

data	autoreplace	off	default
data	cachefile	-	default
data	failmode	wait	default
data	listsnapshots	off	default
data	autoexpand	off	default
data	dedupditto	0	default
data	dedupratio	1.00x	-
data	free	2,59T	-
data	allocated	133G	-
data	readonly	off	-
data	ashift	0	default
data	comment	-	default
data	expandsize	-	-
data	freeing	0	default
data	fragmentation	3%	-
data	leaked	0	default
data	feature@async_destroy	enabled	local
data	feature@empty_bpobj	active	local
data	feature@lz4_compress	active	local
data	feature@spacemap_histogram	active	local
data	feature@enabled_txg	active	local
data	feature@hole_birth	active	local
data	feature@extensible_dataset	enabled	local
data	feature@embedded_data	active	local
data	feature@bookmarks	enabled	local

As you may have noticed, I let ZFS auto-detect the value.

smartctl

If you are unsure about the AL status for your drives, use the smartctl command:

```
[trochej@madtower sohozfs]$ sudo smartctl -a /dev/sda

smartctl 6.4 2015-06-04 r4109 [x86_64-linux-4.4.0] (local build)
Copyright (C) 2002-15, Bruce Allen, Christian Franke,
    www.smartmontools.org

=== START OF INFORMATION SECTION ===
Model Family:     Seagate Laptop SSHD
Device Model:     ST500LM000-1EJ162
Serial Number:    W7622ZRQ
LU WWN Device Id: 5 000c50 07c920424
Firmware Version: DEM9
User Capacity:    500,107,862,016 bytes [500 GB]
Sector Sizes:     512 bytes logical, 4096 bytes physical
Rotation Rate:    5400 rpm
Form Factor:      2.5 inches
Device is:        In smartctl database [for details use: -P show]
ATA Version is:   ACS-2, ACS-3 T13/2161-D revision 3b
SATA Version is:  SATA 3.1, 6.0 Gb/s (current: 6.0 Gb/s)
Local Time is:    Fri Feb 12 22:11:18 2016 CET
SMART support is: Available - device has SMART capability.
SMART support is: Enabled
```

You will notice that my drive has the line:

```
Sector Sizes:     512 bytes logical, 4096 bytes physical
```

It tells us that drive has a physical layout of 4096 bytes, but the driver advertises 512 bytes for backward compatibility.

Deduplication

As a rule of thumb, don't dedupe. Just don't. If you really need to watch out for disk space, use other ways of increasing capacity. Several of my past customers got into very big trouble using deduplication.

ZFS has an interesting option that spurred quite lot of interest when it was introduced. Turning deduplication on tells ZFS to keep track of data blocks. Whenever data is written to disks, ZFS will compare it with the blocks already in the file system and if finds any block identical, it will not write physical data, but will add some meta-information and thus save lots and lots of disk space.

While the feature seems great in theory, in practice it turns out to be rather tricky to use smartly. First of all, deduplication comes at a cost and it's a cost in RAM and CPU power. For each data block that is being deduplicated, your system will add an entry to DDT (deduplication tables) that exist in your RAM. Ironically, for ideally deduplicating data, the result of DDT in RAM was that the system ground to a halt by lack of memory and CPU power for operating system functions.

It is not to say deduplication is without uses. Before you set it though, you should research how well your data would deduplicate. I can envision storage for backups that would conserve space by use of deduplication. In such a case though the size of DDT, free RAM amount and CPU utilization must be observed to avoid problems.

The catch is, DDT are persistent. You can, at any moment, disable deduplication, but once deduplicated data stays deduplicated and if you run into system stability issues due to it, disabling and rebooting won't help. On the next pool import (mount), DDT will be loaded into RAM again. There are two ways to get rid of this data: destroy the pool, create it anew, and restore the data or disable deduplication, or move data on the pool so it gets undeduplicated on the next writes. Both options take time, depending on the size of your data. While deduplication may save disk space, research it carefully.

The deduplication ratio is by default displayed using the zpool list command. A ratio of 1.00 means no deduplication happened:

```
trochej@madchamber:~$ sudo zpool list
```

```
NAME SIZE  ALLOC FREE  EXPANDSZ FRAG CAP DEDUP HEALTH ALTROOT
data 2,72T 133G  2,59T  -        3%   4% 1.00x ONLINE -
```

You can check the deduplication setting by querying your file system's deduplication property:

```
trochej@madchamber:~$ sudo zfs get dedup data/datafs
```

```
NAME          PROPERTY  VALUE       SOURCE
data/datafs   dedup     off         default
```

Deduplication is a setting set per file system.

Compression

An option that saves disk space and adds speed is *compression*. There are several compression algorithms available for use by ZFS. Basically, you can tell the file system to compress any block of data it will write to disk. With modern CPUs, you can usually add some speed by writing smaller physical data. Your processors should be able to cope with packing and unpacking data on the fly. The exception can be data that compress badly, such as MP3s, JPGs, or video file. Textual data (application logs, etc.) usually plays well with this option. For personal use, I always turn it on. The default compression algorithm for ZFS is lzjb.

The compression can be set by on a file system basis:

```
trochej@madchamber:~$ sudo zfs get compression data/datafs
```

```
NAME            PROPERTY      VALUE      SOURCE
data/datafs   compression   on          local
```

```
trochej@madchamber:~$ sudo zfs set compression=on data/datafs
```

The compression ratio can be determined by querying a property:

```
trochej@madchamber:~$ sudo zfs get compressratio data/datafs
```

```
NAME            PROPERTY       VALUE    SOURCE
data/datafs   compressratio   1.26x
```

Several compression algorithms are available. Until recently, if you simply turned compression on, the lzjb algorithm was used. It is considered a good compromise between performance and compression. Other compression algorithms available are listed on the `zfs` man page. A new algorithm added recently is lz4. It has better performance and a higher compression ratio than lzjb. It can only be enabled for pools that have the `feature@lz4_compress` feature flag property:

```
trochej@madchamber:~$ sudo zpool get feature@lz4_compress data
```

```
NAME  PROPERTY             VALUE      SOURCE
data  feature@lz4_compress   active      local
```

If the feature is enabled, you can set `compression=lz4` for any given dataset. You can enable it by invoking this command:

```
trochej@madchamber:~$ sudo zpool set feature@lz4_
compress=enabled data
```

lz4 has been the default compression algorithm for some time now.

ZFS Pool State

If you look again at the listing of my pool:

```
trochej@madchamber:~$ sudo zpool list

NAME SIZE  ALLOC FREE  EXPANDSZ FRAG CAP DEDUP HEALTH ALTROOT
data 2,72T 133G  2,59T -        3%   4%  1.00x ONLINE -
```

You will notice a column called HEALTH. This is a status of the ZFS pool. There are several other indicators that you can see here:

- ONLINE: The pool is healthy (there are no errors detected) and it is imported (mounted in traditional file systems jargon) and ready to use. It doesn't mean it's perfectly okay. ZFS will keep a pool marked online even if some small number of I/O errors or correctable data errors occur. You should monitor other indicators as well such as disk health (hdparm, smartctl, and lsiutil for LSI SAS controllers).

- DEGRADED: Probably only applicable to redundant sets, where disks in mirror or RAIDZ or RAIDZ-2 pools have been lost. The pool may have become non-redundant. Losing more disks may render it corrupt. Bear in mind that in triple-mirror or RAIDZ-2, losing one disk doesn't render a pool non-redundant.

- FAULTED: A disk or a vdev is inaccessible. It means that ZFS cannot read or write to it. In redundant configurations, a disk may be FAULTED but its vdev may be DEGRADED and still accessible. This may happen if in the mirrored set, one disk is lost. If you lose a top-level vdev, i.e., both disks in a mirror, your whole pool will be inaccessible and will become corrupt. Since there is no

way to restore a file system, your options at this stage
are to recreate the pool with healthy disks and restore
it from backups or seek ZFS data recovery experts. The
latter is usually a costly option.

- OFFLINE: A device has been disabled (taken offline) by
  the administrator. Reasons may vary, but it need not
  mean the disk is faulty.

- UNAVAIL: The disk or vdev cannot be opened. Effectively
  ZFS cannot read or write to it. You may notice it sounds
  very similar to FAULTED state. The difference is mainly
  that in the FAULTED state, the device has displayed
  number of errors before being marked as FAULTED by
  ZFS. With UNAVAIL, the system cannot talk to the device;
  possibly it went totally dead or the power supply is too
  weak to power all of your disks. The last scenario is
  something to keep in mind, especially on commodity
  hardware. I've run into dissapearing disks more than
  once, just to figure out that the PSU was too weak.

- REMOVED: If your hardware supports it, when a disk is
  physically removed without first removing it from the
  pool using the zpool command, it will be marked as
  REMOVED.

You can check pool health explicitly using the zpool status and zpool
status -x commands:

```
trochej@madchamber:~$ sudo zpool status -x

all pools are healthy

trochej@madchamber:~$ sudo zpool status
  pool: data
 state: ONLINE
```

```
  scan: none requested
config:

        NAME          STATE     READ WRITE CKSUM
        data          ONLINE       0     0     0
        sdb           ONLINE       0     0     0

errors: No known data errors
```

zpool status will print detailed health and configuration of all the pool devices. When the pool consists of hundreds of disks, it may be troublesome to fish out a faulty device. To that end, you can use zpool status -x, which will print only the status of the pools that experienced issues.

```
trochej@madchamber:~$ sudo zpool status -x

  pool: data
 state: DEGRADED
status: One or more devices has been taken offline by the administrator.
        Sufficient replicas exist for the pool to continue
        functioning in a degraded state.
action: Online the device using 'zpool online' or replace the
        device with 'zpool replace'.
 scrub: resilver completed after 0h0m with 0 errors on Wed Feb
        10 15:15:09 2016
config:

        NAME          STATE     READ WRITE CKSUM
        data          ONLINE       0     0     0
        mirror-0      DEGRADED     0     0     0
        sdb           ONLINE       0     0     0
        sdc           OFFLINE      0     0     0 48K resilvered

errors: No known data errors
```

ZFS Version

ZFS was designed to incrementally introduce new features. As part of that mechanism, the ZFS versions have been introduced by a single number. Tracking that number, the system operator can determine if their pool uses the latest ZFS version, including new features and bug fixes. Upgrades are done in-place and do not require any downtime.

That philosophy was functioning quite well when ZFS was developed solely by Sun Microsystems. With the advent of the OpenZFS community—gathering developers from illumos, Linux, OSX, and FreeBSD worlds—it soon became obvious that it would be difficult if not impossible to agree with every on-disk format change across the whole community. Thus, the version number stayed at the latest that was ever released as open source from Oracle Corp: 28. From that point, pluggable architecture of "features flags" was introduced. ZFS implementations are compatible if they implement the same set of feature flags.

If you look again at the `zpool` command output for my host:

```
trochej@madchamber:~$ sudo zpool get all data
```

NAME	PROPERTY	VALUE	SOURCE
data	size	2,72T	-
data	capacity	4%	-
data	altroot	-	default
data	health	ONLINE	-
data	guid	7057182016879104894	default
data	version	-	default
data	bootfs	-	default
data	delegation	on	default
data	autoreplace	off	default
data	cachefile	-	default
data	failmode	wait	default

data	listsnapshots	off	default
data	autoexpand	off	default
data	dedupditto	0	default
data	dedupratio	1.00x	-
data	free	2,59T	-
data	allocated	133G	-
data	readonly	off	-
data	ashift	0	default
data	comment	-	default
data	expandsize	-	-
data	freeing	0	default
data	fragmentation	3%	-
data	leaked	0	default
data	feature@async_destroy	enabled	local
data	feature@empty_bpobj	active	local
data	feature@lz4_compress	active	local
data	feature@spacemap_histogram	active	local
data	feature@enabled_txg	active	local
data	feature@hole_birth	active	local
data	feature@extensible_dataset	enabled	local
data	feature@embedded_data	active	local
data	feature@bookmarks	enabled	local

You will notice that last few properties start with the feature@ string. That's the feature flags you need to look for. The find out the all supported versions and feature flags, run the sudo zfs upgrade -v and sudo zpool upgrade -v commands, as shown in the following examples:

```
trochej@madchamber:~$ sudo zfs upgrade -v
```

The following file system versions are supported:

```
VER   DESCRIPTION
---   -----------------------------------------------------------
 1    Initial ZFS file system version
 2    Enhanced directory entries
 3    Case insensitive and file system user identifier (FUID)
 4    userquota, groupquota properties
 5    System attributes
```

For more information on a particular version, including supported releases, see the ZFS Administration Guide.

```
trochej@madchamber:~$ sudo zpool upgrade -v
```

This system supports ZFS pool feature flags.

The following features are supported:

```
FEAT DESCRIPTION
-------------------------------------------------------------
async_destroy                         (read-only compatible)
     Destroy file systems asynchronously.
empty_bpobj                           (read-only compatible)
     Snapshots use less space.
lz4_compress
     LZ4 compression algorithm support.
spacemap_histogram                    (read-only compatible)
     Spacemaps maintain space histograms.
enabled_txg                           (read-only compatible)
     Record txg at which a feature is enabled
hole_birth
     Retain hole birth txg for more precise zfs send
extensible_dataset
     Enhanced dataset functionality, used by other features.
```

embedded_data

    Blocks which compress very well use even less space.

bookmarks   (read-only compatible)

    "zfs bookmark" command

The following legacy versions are also supported:

VER DESCRIPTION

--- --

1   Initial ZFS version

2   Ditto blocks (replicated metadata)

3   Hot spares and double parity RAID-Z

4   zpool history

5   Compression using the gzip algorithm

6   bootfs pool property

7   Separate intent log devices

8   Delegated administration

9   refquota and refreservation properties

10   Cache devices

11   Improved scrub performance

12   Snapshot properties

13   snapused property

14   passthrough-x aclinherit

15   user/group space accounting

16   stmf property support

17   Triple-parity RAID-Z

18   Snapshot user holds

19   Log device removal

20   Compression using zle (zero-length encoding)

21   Deduplication

22   Received properties

23   Slim ZIL

24   System attributes

```
25  Improved scrub stats
26  Improved snapshot deletion performance
27  Improved snapshot creation performance
28  Multiple vdev replacements
```

For more information on a particular version, including supported releases, see the ZFS Administration Guide.

Both commands print information on a maximum level of ZFS pool and file system versions and list the available feature flags .

You can check the current version of your pool and file systems using the zpool upgrade and zfs upgrade commands:

trochej@madchamber:~$ sudo zpool upgrade

This system supports ZFS pool feature flags.

All pools are formatted using feature flags.

Every feature flags pool has all supported features enabled.

trochej@madchamber:~$ sudo zfs upgrade

This system is currently running ZFS file system version 5.

All file systems are formatted with the current version.

Linux is a dominant operating system in the server area. ZFS is a very good file system for storage in most scenarios. Compared to traditional RAID and volume management solutions, it brings several advantages—simplicity of use, data healing capabilities, improved ability to migrate between operating systems, and many more. ZFS deals with virtual devices (*vdevs*). Virtual device can be either mapped directly to physical disk or to a grouping of other vdevs. A group of vdevs that serve as space for file systems is called a *ZFS pool.* The file systems within them are called file systems. ZFS file systems can be nested. Administrating the pool is done by the zpool command. Administration of file systems is done by the zfs command.

CHAPTER 2

Hardware

Before you buy hardware for your storage, there are a few things to consider. How much disk space will you need? How many client connections (sessions) will your storage serve? Which protocol will you use? What kind of data do you plan to serve?

Don't Rush

The first piece of advice that you always should keep in mind: don't rush it. You are about to invest your money and time. While you can later modify the storage according to your needs, some changes will require that you recreate the ZFS pool, which means all data on it will be lost. If you buy the wrong disks (e.g., they are too small), you will need to add more and may run out of free slots or power.

Considerations

There are a few questions you should ask yourself before starting to scope the storage. Answers that you give here will play a key role in later deployment.

© Damian Wojsław 2017
D. Wojsław, *Introducing ZFS on Linux*, https://doi.org/10.1007/978-1-4842-3306-1_2

How Much Data?

The amount of data you expect to store will determine the number and size of disks you need to buy. It will also affect other factors, such as server size. To scope your space needs you would need to assess how much data you currently have and how quickly it grows. Consider how long you are going to run the storage you are building. It may be that you plan to replace it completely in three years and thus don't have to be very careful. It may be you don't know when new storage will be implemented and thus need to add some margin. Look at your organisation growth plans. Are you going to double number of office personnell within three years? Are they all going to produce data? That would mean three years from now data will grow at least three times as quick as currently.

How Many Concurrent Clients?

The number of concurrent client connections determines the amount of RAM that you'll need. You could buy SSD disks to serve as level 2 cache for your storage and resign from using SATA disk at all, if you were considering them. Even if you are going to store hundreds of terabytes, but only a few client machines will ever utilize it and not very intensively, you may be able to get by with a low amount of memory. This will also determine the kind of network interface in your server and the kind of switch it should be attached to.

How Critical Is the Data?

How critical is your data? If it's mission-critical, look at certified and probably more costly hardware, known to perform well and for a longer time. The importance of your data will also tell you which redundancy level you should use, which influences the final cost. My personal experience from various data centers suggests that SATA disks are failing much faster than SAS.

What Types of Data?

The kind of data you will serve may affect the architecture of your storage pool. Streaming video files for a considerable number of clients or servicing virtual machines and data files will most probably mean you need to use mirrors, which directly influence the final capacity of your array and final cost.

What Kind of Scope?

First, create an upper bounds for what will be considered SoHo storage in this guide:

- Given your current disk sizes, up to 12 slots in a single node, and up to 30 TB of raw capacity.

- Either internal SAS or SATA drives.

- One or two slots for eventual SSDs for speeding up reads.

- Possibly a mirrored ZIL device to speed up and concatenate writes to disks. A system drive, possibly mirrored, although currently setting up Linux system on ZFS is not trivial and booting from ZFS is not recommended.

- Up to 128 GB of RAM, possibly 64.

- A 64-bit CPU with four or more cores. While running ZFS on 32-bit systems is possible, it certainly is not recommended.

If you intend to use external disk enclosures (JBODS) connected through SAS or FibreChannel, this book is probably not intended for you. It is possible to set up and administer such storage manually and many people have done so, but it may involve additional steps not covered in the guide. If you want to run tens or hundreds of disks, do yourself a favor and consider FreeNAS or even commercial solutions with paid support. Keeping track of system performance, memory usage, disks, controllers, and cable health is probably best managed by specialized products.

Hardware Purchase Guidelines

Hardware is usually a long-term investment. Try to remember the following points.

Same Vendor, Different Batch

When buying disks, a common practice is to make sure you buy each disk from the same vendor and model, to keep geometry and firmware the same, but from different batches, so you minimize the risk of several disks dying at the same time. I suppose that for a small-time buyer (a few up to 20 disks), the simplest way to achieve it is to buy disks from different shops. Might be cumbersome, but storage operators have seen disk batches failing at the same time many times in their lives.

Buy a Few Pieces for Spares

Storage system lifetime is usually counted in years and is often longer than a disk model, especially if you decide to use consumer-grade SATA disks. When one of them fails in a few years, you may be surprised by the fact that you cannot buy this model any more. Introducing a different one in a pool is always a performance risk. If that happens, don't despair. ZFS lets you exchange all disks in a pool. This trick has been used in the past to increase the size of the pool when it became insufficient. Be aware that replacing all disks in a 10-disk pool can take weeks on a filled and busy system.

Scope Power Supply Properly

If your power unit is unstable or insufficient, you may encounter mysterious failures (disks disappearing, disk connection dropping, or random I/O errors to the pool) or may not be able to use your disks at all.

Consider Performance, Plan for RAM

Performance-wise, the more disks the better. The smaller disks, the better. ZFS threads writes and reads among vdevs. The more vdevs, the more read/write threads. Plan for much RAM. ZFS needs at least 2 GB of RAM to work sensibly, but for any real-life use, don't go below 8 GB. For a storage system for SoHo, I recommend looking at 64 GB or more. ZFS caches data very aggressively, so it will try to use as much RAM as possible. It will, however, yield when the system demands RAM for normal operations (such as new programs being run). So the more it can fit in your memory, the better.

Plan for SSDs (At Least Three)

You don't need to buy them upfront. ZFS is a hybrid storage file system, which means that it can use SSD disks for the level 2 cache. It's gonna be much slower than you RAM, but it's cheaper and still much faster than your platter disks. For a fraction of the RAM price, you can get a 512 GB SSD drive, which should allow for another speed improvement. That's one SSD. Two SSDs would be for an external ZFS Intent Log. The file system doesn't flush all the data all the time to physical storage. It ties writes in transactions and flushes several at the same time, to minimize file system fragmentation and real I/O to disks.

If you give ZFS external devices for ZIL, it can speed things up by grouping even more data before flushing it down. This additional pool device should be mirrored, because it's where you can lose your data.

In case of power failure, data on external ZIL must be persistent. There are battery backed-up DRAM devices that emulate small SSD disks, i.e., ZeusRAM. They come in 8 and 16 GB sizes, which is enough for ZIL. They are fast as memory, but they are costly. You can think of mirroring your L2ARC too (the level 2 cache), but losing this device won't endanger your data.

Consider SATA

While the SAS standard is sure to get better performance and life expectancy from your disks, for SoHo solutions SATA is enough, especially if you consider that there are enterprise-class SATA disks. The price difference for such deployment shouldn't be very high. If you're unsure, choose SAS if your budget allows.

Do Not Buy Hardware and Soft RAID Controllers

While in the past, RAID cards were necessary to offload both CPU units and RAM, both of those resources are now abundant and cheap. You CPU and your RAM will be more than enough for the workload and RAID cards take away one important capability of ZFS. ZFS ensures data safety by talking directly to the disk: getting reliable information on when data is flushed to physical disks and what block sizes are being used.

RAID controllers mediate in between and can make their own "optimizations" to the I/O, which may lower ZFS reliability. The other thing is, RAID controllers are incompatible between various vendors and even the same card but different firmware revision may be unable to access your RAID set. This means that in case of controller failure, you lose the whole setup and need to restore data from a backup. Soft RAIDs are even worse, in that they need special software (often limited to only one operating system) to actually work.

ZFS is superior in all of these areas. Not only can it use all processing power and all RAM you can give it to speed up your I/O, but the disks in the pool can also be migrated between all software platforms that implement the same OpenZFS version. Also, the exact sequence of disks in disk slots is not important, as the pool remembers its configuration based on disk device names (i.e., /dev/sdb) as well as by the disk GUID given them by ZFS during pool creation.

Networking Cards at Least 1 GB of Speed

Remember that this server networking card's bandwidth will be spread among all the machines that will simultaneously utilize the storage. It is quite sensible to consider 10 GB, but you also need to consider your other networking gear—switches, cabling, etc. Remember that the network plays a role in performance analysis and quite a large amount of performance issues are caused not by the storage itself, but by the networking layer. For serious work in an office I would suggest going no lower than 10GB network cards. 1GB are acceptable in a very small environment where storage won't be used extensively. Anything less will quickly become inconvenient at best.

Plan for Redundancy

Always. This means that for high-speed read pools, you need to consider mirrored storage, effectively halving total capacity of the disks you buy. RAIDZ setup means your capacity will be lowered by one disk per each vdev you create. For RAIDZ-2, it will be two disks.

Data Security

You are going to use ZFS storage to keep data and serve it to various people in your company. Be it two, ten, or fifty people, always put some thought into planning the layout. Various directories that will store data that vary by kind, sensitivity, and compressibility will pay off in the future. Well-designed directory structure will simplify both organizational things, like access control and the technical side, like enabled or disabled compression, time options, etc.

ZFS file systems behave like directories. It is quite common to create a separate ZFS file system per the user home directory, for example, so that they can have fine-grained backup policies, ACLs, and compression mechanisms.

You need to consider your company size, number of employees accessing the storage, growth perspectives, data sensitivity, etc. Whatever you do, however, don't skip this point. I've seen quite a few companies that overlooked the moment they needed to switch from an infrastructure that freely evolves into something that is engineered.

CIA

There are many data security methodologies and one of them, I believe the most classic, uses the acronym CIA to explain aspects of data security. This stands for Confidentiality, Integrity, and Availability. While it focuses rather on the InfoSec side of things, it's a pretty good view of storage administration also. The next sections introduce these concepts from the point of view of the storage administrator.

Confidentiality

Data must be available only to people who are entrusted with it. No one who is not explicitly allowed to view data should be able to access it. This side of security is covered by many infrastructural tools, from policies and NDAs that people allowed to view data should read and sign, through network access separation (VPNs, VLANs, access control through credentials). There are also aspects directly related to storage itself: Access Control Lists (ACLs), sharing through secure protocols and in secure networks, working with storage firewalls, etc.

Integrity

It must be guaranteed that the data is genuine and was not changed by people who are not entrusted. Also, the change should not be introduced by software or hardware, intentionally or not, if it's not supposed to. Through the whole data lifecycle, only people with sufficient privileges should be allowed to modify the data. Unintentional data integrity breaches may be a disk failure that breaks data blocks. While with text data it is usually easily spotted, with other data, like sound or video, it's harder because there can be subtle differences from the original state. As with all aspects of security, it's also only partially administered by storage. The data integrity is covered by ACLs, but also by ZFS checksumming data blocks to detect corruption. If your setup uses any redundancy, ZFS can, to great extent, fix those for you using the redundant set.

Availability

The data should be available at all times it is required and guaranteed. This is probably one of most obvious aspects of storage. Any time you expect your data should be up, the data should be up. Typically, storage redundancy comes into play here (mirror, RAIDZ, and RAIDZ-2), but so do network cards trunking, switch stacking, and the redundancy of any credentials checking solution you are using (Active Directory server, primary and secondary, for example).

Types of Workload

The workload you are going to run on the storage will play a major role in how you should plan the pool layout.

If you are going to mostly host databases and they are going to be the dominating consumers of the space, L2ARC SSD device may not provide you with special performance gains. Databases are very good at caching their own data and if it so happens that the data fits into the database server RAM, ARC will not have much to do. On the other hand, if the data in your database change often and needs to be reread from disks, you are going to have high miss ratio anyway and, again, the L2ARC device will not fulfill its purpose.

The snapshotting data is also going to be tricky. Databases need lots more than a snapshot of the file system to be able to work on the data. This is why they come with their own dump commands—because the full working backup usually contains more than what lives in the database files. Hosting a database would usually mean you run the engine on the same host as your ZFS. Again, the database will use the RAM more efficiently than the file system itself. Consider though, if you will serve data from the same server for other purposes, such as CIFS or NFS share. In that case, the database and file system cache may compete for RAM. While this shouldn't affect the system stability, it may adversely affect performance.

If you host documents and pictures for office workers, files like procedures, and technical documentations, a L2ARC device is something to seriously consider. Snapshotting is then a reliable way of capturing data at certain points in time. If your data is not being accessed 24 hours a day and you can have just a few seconds of off-time, a snapshot can reliably host your data at a specified point of time. It usually takes about a second to create. You can later mount this snapshot—remember it is read-only—and transfer it to a backup location, not worrying about data integrity.

Above all, don't rush it. You can always add L2ARC later on to your pool, if performance tests prove to be unsatisfactory.

Other Components To Pay Attention To

It is important to pay attention to other infrastructure elements. The network is of special interest. In a small company of a few persons, a small switch with the workstation refit as a storage server might perform without any issue, but once the number of data consumers starts to grow, this kind of network may soon become a bottleneck. Switches may not be the only limiting factor. Network cards in your storage server may prove to be another one. Also, if you serve your data over VPNs from a remote location, it may turn out that the interlink is too slow. Quite often on a storage performance analysis case, we were able to point to networking infrastructure as the faulty element.

Hardware Checklist

Don't rush. Before buying your hardware, sit down with a piece of paper or with your laptop and make a list. Think about how much space you will need and how this need may grow in several years. Think about your budget. How much you can spend? Count the number of machines you will be connecting to the storage and describe the kind of traffic that will be served. Lots of small files? Big, several gigabyte-sized files? Plan some tests and assume you'll need a few days to make them.

CHAPTER 3

Installation

This chapter goes through the basic installation of ZFS modules in your
Linux distribution of choice. Ubuntu allows for quick install and setup, so
we are going to use it as an example.

System Packages

Before going any further, you need to install some packages from the
standard distribution repositories.

Virtual Machine

Before buying the hardware and running tests on bare metal, you may
want to install and test ZFS within a virtual machine. It is a good idea and
I encourage you to do so. You may, in a very simple and efficient way, get
used to administering ZFS pools. You may also check which distribution
works better for you. There are no requirements to the virtualization
engine. You can use VirtualBox, VMware, KVM, Xen, or any other VM you
feel comfortable with. Keep in mind that the tool you use should be able to
provide your guest machine with virtual disks to play with. While you can
create a pool on the files created within the VM, I don't recommend that
way of testing it.

© Damian Wojsław 2017
D. Wojsław, *Introducing ZFS on Linux*, https://doi.org/10.1007/978-1-4842-3306-1_3

Note   Bear in mind that virtual machines are not suitable for performance testing. Too many factors stand in the way of reliable results.

Ubuntu Server

If, for some reason, you are running Ubuntu prior to 15.10, you will need to add a special PPA repository:

```
trochej@ubuntuzfs:~$ sudo add-apt-repository ppa:zfs-native/
stable

[sudo] password for trochej:
 The native ZFS filesystem for Linux. Install the ubuntu-zfs
package.

Please join this Launchpad user group if you want to show
support for ZoL:

  https://launchpad.net/~zfs-native-users

Send feedback or requests for help to this email list:

  http://list.zfsonlinux.org/mailman/listinfo/zfs-discuss

Report bugs at:

  https://github.com/zfsonlinux/zfs/issues  (for the driver itself)
  https://github.com/zfsonlinux/pkg-zfs/issues (for the packaging)

The ZoL project home page is:

  http://zfsonlinux.org/
```

More info: https://launchpad.net/~zfs-native/+archive/ubuntu/
stable

Press [ENTER] to **continue** or ctrl-c to cancel adding it

```
gpg: keyring `/tmp/tmp4_wvpmaf/secring.gpg' created
gpg: keyring `/tmp/tmp4_wvpmaf/pubring.gpg' created
gpg: requesting key F6B0FC61 from hkp server keyserver.ubuntu.com
gpg: /tmp/tmp4_wvpmaf/trustdb.gpg: trustdb created
gpg: key F6B0FC61: public key "Launchpad PPA for Native ZFS for
    Linux" imported
gpg: Total number processed: 1
gpg:                  imported: 1  (RSA: 1)
OK
```

With Ubuntu 15.10 and later, ZFS support packages are already
included in the standard repository. You will need to install the following
packages:

```
trochej@ubuntuzfs:~$ sudo apt-get install zfsutils-linux
```

This will compile the appropriate kernel modules for you. You can later
confirm that they were built and in fact loaded by running lsmod:

```
trochej@ubuntuzfs:~$ sudo lsmod | grep zfs

zfs              2252800  0
zunicode          331776  1 zfs
zcommon            53248  1 zfs
znvpair            90112  2 zfs,zcommon
spl               102400  3 zfs,zcommon,znvpair
zavl               16384  1 zfs
```

You should be now able to create a pool:

```
trochej@ubuntuzfs:~$ sudo zpool create -f datapool \
    mirror /dev/sdb /dev/sdc \
    mirror /dev/sdd /dev/sde \
    mirror /dev/sdf /dev/sdg

trochej@ubuntuzfs:~$ sudo zpool status
  pool: datapool
 state: ONLINE
  scan: none requested
config:

    NAME          STATE      READ WRITE CKSUM
    datapool      ONLINE        0     0     0
      mirror-0    ONLINE        0     0     0
        sdb       ONLINE        0     0     0
        sdc       ONLINE        0     0     0
      mirror-1    ONLINE        0     0     0
        sdd       ONLINE        0     0     0
        sde       ONLINE        0     0     0
      mirror-2    ONLINE        0     0     0
        sdf       ONLINE        0     0     0
        sdg       ONLINE        0     0     0

errors: No known data errors
```

There is another package you will want to install:

```
trochej@ubuntuzfs:~$ sudo apt-get install zfs-zed
```

zed is a *ZFS Event Daemon*. It is a daemon service that will listen to any ZFS-generated kernel event. It's explained in more detail in the next section.

CentOS

You will need a system information tool that is not installed by default for monitoring, troubleshooting, and testing your setup:

[root@localhost ~]# *yum install sysstat*

Contrary to Ubuntu, CentOS doesn't have ZFS packages by default in the repository, neither in its 6.7 nor 7 version. Thus you need to follow the directions here: http://zfsonlinux.org/epel.html.

The installation for CentOS 7 is exactly the same, except for the package names:

[root@CentosZFS ~]# *yum localinstall --nogpgcheck https://download.fedoraproject.org/pub/epel/6/x86_64/epel-release-6-8.noarch.rpm*
[root@CentosZFS ~]# *yum localinstall --nogpgcheck http://archive.zfsonlinux.org/epel/zfs-release.el6.noarch.rpm*
[root@CentosZFS ~]# *yum install -y kernel-devel zfs*

After some time, you should be ready to probe and use ZFS modules:

```
[root@CentosZFS ~]# modprobe zfs
[root@CentosZFS ~]# lsmod | grep zfs
zfs             2735595  0
zcommon           48128  1 zfs
znvpair           80220  2 zfs,zcommon
spl               90378  3 zfs,zcommon,znvpair
zavl               7215  1 zfs
zunicode         323046  1 zfs
```

You're now ready to create a pool on your attached disks:

```
[root@CentosZFS ~]# zpool create -f datapool mirror /dev/sdb /
dev/sdc mirror /dev/sdd /dev/sde
[root@CentosZFS ~]# zpool status
  pool: datapool
 state: ONLINE
  scan: none requested
 config:

    NAME        STATE     READ WRITE CKSUM
    datapool    ONLINE       0     0     0
      mirror-0  ONLINE       0     0     0
        sdb     ONLINE       0     0     0
        sdc     ONLINE       0     0     0
      mirror-1  ONLINE       0     0     0
        sdd     ONLINE       0     0     0
        sde     ONLINE       0     0     0

errors: No known data errors
```

This code installed the aforementioned ZED for you.

System Tools

You will need some system tools. Get used to them.

- smartctl: The smartmontools package contains two
  utility programs (smartctl and smartd) to control and
  monitor storage systems. It uses the Self-Monitoring,
  Analysis, and Reporting Technology System (SMART)
  built into most modern ATA/SATA, SCSI/SAS, and
  NVMe disks.

- lsblk: Tells you what block devices you have. It will assist you in identifying the drive names you will use while setting your ZFS pool.

- blkid: Helps you identify drives already used by other file systems. You may want to use mount and df for that purpose too.

ZED

As mentioned, zed is a daemon that will listen to kernel events related to ZFS. Upon receiving events, it will conduct any action defined in so-called ZEDLETs—a script or program that will carry on whatever action it's supposed to do. ZED is a Linux-specific daemon. In illumos distributions, FMA is the layer responsible for carrying out corrective actions.

Writing ZEDLETs is a topic beyond this guide, but the daemon is essential for two important tasks: monitoring and reporting (via mail) pool health and replacing failed drives with hot spares.

Even though it is a ZFS that is responsible for marking a drive as faulty, the replacement action needs to be carried out by a separate entity.

For those actions to work, after installing the daemon, open its configuration file. It's usually found in /etc/zfs/zed.d/zed.rc:

 # zed.rc

 # Absolute path to the debug output file.
 # ZED_DEBUG_LOG="/tmp/zed.debug.log"

 # Email address of the zpool administrator.
 #   Email will only be sent if ZED_EMAIL is defined.
ZED_EMAIL="admin@example.net"

 # Email verbosity.
 #   If set to 0, suppress email if the pool is healthy.

 #   If set to 1, send email regardless of pool health.
#ZED_EMAIL_VERBOSE=0

 # Minimum number of seconds between emails sent for a similar event.
#ZED_EMAIL_INTERVAL_SECS="3600"

 # Default directory for zed lock files.
#ZED_LOCKDIR="/var/lock"

 # Default directory for zed state files.
#ZED_RUNDIR="/var/run"

 # The syslog priority (eg, specified as a "facility.level" pair).
ZED_SYSLOG_PRIORITY="daemon.notice"

 # The syslog tag for marking zed events.
ZED_SYSLOG_TAG="zed"

 # Replace a device with a hot spare after N I/O errors are detected.
#ZED_SPARE_ON_IO_ERRORS=1

 # Replace a device with a hot spare after N checksum errors are
  detected.
#ZED_SPARE_ON_CHECKSUM_ERRORS=10

Notice ZED_EMAIL, ZED_SPARE_ON_IO_ERRORS, and ZED_SPARE_ON_
CHECKSUM_ERRORS. Uncomment them if you want this functionality.

You can view the kernel messages that zed will listen to by using zpool
events with or without the -v switch. Without the switch, you will receive a
list similar to this one:

```
trochej@ubuntuzfs:~$ sudo zpool events
TIME                            CLASS
Feb 15 2016 17:43:08.213103724 resource.fs.zfs.statechange
```

```
Feb 15 2016 17:43:08.221103592 resource.fs.zfs.statechange
Feb 15 2016 17:43:08.221103592 resource.fs.zfs.statechange
Feb 15 2016 17:43:08.661096327 ereport.fs.zfs.config.sync
Feb 15 2016 18:07:39.521832629 ereport.fs.zfs.zpool.destroy
```

Those should be pretty obvious and, in this case, it's directly related to creation, import, and destruction of a pool.

With the -v switch, the output is more verbose:

```
trochej@ubuntuzfs:~$ sudo zpool events -v
TIME                            CLASS
Feb 15 2016 17:43:08.213103724 resource.fs.zfs.statechange
    version = 0x0
    class = "resource.fs.zfs.statechange"
    pool_guid = 0xa5c256340cb6bcbc
    pool_context = 0x0
    vdev_guid = 0xba85b9116783d317
    vdev_state = 0x7
    time = 0x56c2001c 0xcb3b46c
    eid = 0xa

Feb 15 2016 17:43:08.213103724 resource.fs.zfs.statechange
    version = 0x0
    class = "resource.fs.zfs.statechange"
    pool_guid = 0xa5c256340cb6bcbc
    pool_context = 0x0
    vdev_guid = 0xbcb660041118eb95
    vdev_state = 0x7
    time = 0x56c2001c 0xcb3b46c
    eid = 0xb
```

CHAPTER 4

Setup

We've already presented various pool layout performance issues, so now it's time to consider rules of thumb for the given redundancy types.

> **Note** We won't be covering striped pools. A *striped* pool is a pool consisting of two or more disks that provide no redundancy. While the total pool capacity equals the combined capacity of all the disks in the pool, the file system will become corrupted and subject to data recovery if you lose a single drive. A rule of thumb for storage is: don't use striped pools.

General Considerations

For mirrored pools, a good rule of thumb is to use them only when you really need an incredible read performance or are paranoid about your storage. Disks don't fail that often and a mirrored pool will halve your total pool capacity. With triple mirrors, your capacity will be the total disk's capacity divided by three, and so on. A rule of thumb is to use them sparingly and with care.

© Damian Wojsław 2017
D. Wojsław, *Introducing ZFS on Linux*, https://doi.org/10.1007/978-1-4842-3306-1_4

For RAIDZ (which is a rough equivalent of RAID-5 and RAID-6), go rather for RAIDZ-2. It gives you quite good resilience while conserving a lot of space. There is also another recommendation and from personal experience I'd adhere to it: for RAIDZ pools, have 2n+1 disks per vdev. That's three, five, seven, etc., but no more than eleven. This is 2n data disks plus 1 disk for parity data.

With the smallest set of three disks per vdev, you have basically a capacity of a mirrored set with lower read performance. Consider starting with five disks per vdev. For RAIDZ-2, the rule is to use 2x+2 disks, which translates to four, six, eight, etc., and have no more than 12 disks within a vdev. Given this guide, have a typical target maximum of 20 disks in the pool (including ZIL and L2ARC). It's a good idea to have two eight disks RAIDZ-2 vdevs in the pool, totaling 16 disks of total pool capacity of 12 disks.

Creating a Mirrored Pool

Since I've shown you how to create simple pools in previous chapters, there is no need to demonstrate this now. I am therefore going to jump straight to more involved configurations. Bear in mind, however, that with a single node, the setup options are limited.

As a reminder, we are not going to cover striped pools at all. Your pool will have absolutely no resiliency in such a setup and you should never consider hosting data you care for using such a configuration.

Before running any command that may endanger your data, especially in production, i.e., `zpool create` or `zpool destroy`, confirm that the disks you want to use are those that you intended to be used by ZFS.

We have already covered a simple mirrored pool, so let's create bigger one consisting of 10 disks. I am going to follow with `zpool status` to print the resulting pool configuration:

```
trochej@ubuntuzfs:~$ sudo zpool create -f datapool mirror /dev/
sdb /dev/sdc \
mirror /dev/sdd /dev/sde \
mirror /dev/sdf /dev/sdg \
mirror /dev/sdh /dev/sdi \
mirror /dev/sdj /dev/sdk

trochej@ubuntuzfs:~$ sudo zpool status

  pool: datapool
 state: ONLINE
  scan: none requested
config:
```

NAME	STATE	READ	WRITE	CKSUM
datapool	ONLINE	0	0	0
mirror-0	ONLINE	0	0	0
sdb	ONLINE	0	0	0
sdc	ONLINE	0	0	0
mirror-1	ONLINE	0	0	0
sdd	ONLINE	0	0	0
sde	ONLINE	0	0	0
mirror-2	ONLINE	0	0	0
sdf	ONLINE	0	0	0
sdg	ONLINE	0	0	0
mirror-3	ONLINE	0	0	0
sdh	ONLINE	0	0	0
sdi	ONLINE	0	0	0
mirror-4	ONLINE	0	0	0
sdj	ONLINE	0	0	0
sdk	ONLINE	0	0	0

```
errors: No known data errors
```

The resulting pool total capacity equals half the capacity of all the disks in the pool:

```
trochej@ubuntuzfs:~$ sudo zpool list

NAME       SIZE  ALLOC   FREE  EXPANDSZ   FRAG    CAP
DEDUP  HEALTH  ALTROOT
datapool  9.92G    64K  9.92G         -     0%     0%
1.00x  ONLINE  -
```

The pool is mounted at /datapool and contains a file system called datapool, as you can see in the following output:

```
trochej@ubuntuzfs:~$ sudo zfs list

NAME        USED  AVAIL  REFER  MOUNTPOINT
datapool     58K  9.77G    19K  /datapool
```

Creating a RAIDZ Pool

I am reusing the same disks in all the examples. Before creating a new pool on them, I am going to run zpool destroy on the pool. It does exactly that: it marks a pool as destroyed and disks as free to be used by other ZFS setups. When ZFS adds a disk to the pool, it labels it with its own GUID and some information that allows ZFS to be self-contained. You may move the pool around, export it from the current server, reinstall the server to FreeBSD, and import the same pool without a problem. Thus, if you decide you no longer need the pool and try to reuse disks for other configuration, zpool will refuse to add it to a new one without using the -f switch.

```
trochej@ubuntuzfs:~$ sudo zpool destroy datapool

[sudo] password for trochej:
```

The virtual machine I am working with has 12 disks for use as storage:

```
trochej@ubuntuzfs:~$ ls -ahl /dev/sd[a-z]

brw-rw---- 1 root disk 8,   0 Feb 12 21:59 /dev/sda
brw-rw---- 1 root disk 8,  16 Feb 15 17:43 /dev/sdb
brw-rw---- 1 root disk 8,  32 Feb 15 17:43 /dev/sdc
brw-rw---- 1 root disk 8,  48 Feb 15 17:43 /dev/sdd
brw-rw---- 1 root disk 8,  64 Feb 15 17:43 /dev/sde
brw-rw---- 1 root disk 8,  80 Feb 15 17:43 /dev/sdf
brw-rw---- 1 root disk 8,  96 Feb 15 17:43 /dev/sdg
brw-rw---- 1 root disk 8, 112 Feb 15 17:43 /dev/sdh
brw-rw---- 1 root disk 8, 128 Feb 15 17:43 /dev/sdi
brw-rw---- 1 root disk 8, 144 Feb 15 17:43 /dev/sdj
brw-rw---- 1 root disk 8, 160 Feb 15 17:43 /dev/sdk
brw-rw---- 1 root disk 8, 176 Feb 12 21:59 /dev/sdl
brw-rw---- 1 root disk 8, 192 Feb 12 21:59 /dev/sdm
```

/dev/sda is a system disk, which leaves us with disks from /dev/sdb to /dev/sdm. It means 12 disks for use as storage. Let's create a RAIDZ pool following the previously noted best practice of five disks per vdev:

```
trochej@ubuntuzfs:~$ sudo zpool create datapool \

        raidz /dev/sdb /dev/sdc \
        /dev/sdd /dev/sde /dev/sdf \
        raidz /dev/sdg /dev/sdh \
        /dev/sdi /dev/sdj /dev/sdk

trochej@ubuntuzfs:~$ sudo zpool status

  pool: datapool
 state: ONLINE
  scan: none requested
config:
```

NAME	STATE	READ	WRITE	CKSUM
datapool	ONLINE	0	0	0
raidz1-0	ONLINE	0	0	0
sdb	ONLINE	0	0	0
sdc	ONLINE	0	0	0
sdd	ONLINE	0	0	0
sde	ONLINE	0	0	0
sdf	ONLINE	0	0	0
raidz1-1	ONLINE	0	0	0
sdg	ONLINE	0	0	0
sdh	ONLINE	0	0	0
sdi	ONLINE	0	0	0
sdj	ONLINE	0	0	0
sdk	ONLINE	0	0	0

```
errors: No known data errors

trochej@ubuntuzfs:~$ sudo zpool list
```

NAME	SIZE	ALLOC	FREE	EXPANDSZ	FRAG	CAP	DEDUP	HEALTH	ALTROOT
datapool	19.8G	106K	19.7G	-	0%	0%	1.00x	ONLINE	-

The setup shown here can withstand losing a single disk per each vdev at once. With two disks unused, you can add so-called *hot spares*. Hot spares are idle disks added to a pool for replacement in case any active disk in the pool fails. The replacement is done automatically by ZFS. The hot spare mechanism isn't intelligent, so it can cause resiliency issues if you care for the physical layout of your pool—spread your pool's disks in different JBODs so that you can the lose the whole chassis and still retain the pool and data.

In a simple single server setup, this problem isn't significant. You should be safe adding the spare disk to a pool. I'll demonstrate this process in Chapter 5.

Creating a RAIDZ2 Pool

Let's now walk through creating a RAIDZ2 pool, which will consist of 12 disks spread evenly between two vdevs:

```
trochej@ubuntuzfs:~$ sudo zpool create -f datapool \

    raidz2 /dev/sdb /dev/sdc /dev/sdd \
    /dev/sde /dev/sdf /dev/sdg \
    raidz2 /dev/sdh /dev/sdi /dev/sdj \
    /dev/sdk /dev/sdl /dev/sdm

trochej@ubuntuzfs:~$ sudo zpool status

  pool: datapool
 state: ONLINE
  scan: none requested
config:

        NAME        STATE     READ WRITE CKSUM
        datapool    ONLINE       0     0     0
          raidz2-0  ONLINE       0     0     0
            sdb     ONLINE       0     0     0
            sdc     ONLINE       0     0     0
            sdd     ONLINE       0     0     0
            sde     ONLINE       0     0     0
            sdf     ONLINE       0     0     0
            sdg     ONLINE       0     0     0
          raidz2-1  ONLINE       0     0     0
            sdh     ONLINE       0     0     0
```

```
            sdi     ONLINE      0    0    0
            sdj     ONLINE      0    0    0
            sdk     ONLINE      0    0    0
            sdl     ONLINE      0    0    0
            sdm     ONLINE      0    0    0

errors: No known data errors

trochej@ubuntuzfs:~$ sudo zpool list

NAME      SIZE  ALLOC   FREE  EXPANDSZ   FRAG   CAP  DEDUP
HEALTH  ALTROOT
datapool  23.8G  152K  23.7G        -     0%    0%  1.00x
ONLINE  -
```

Forcing Operations

There are situations where you will want to conduct two operations with final consequences—such as destroying a pool or forcing an operation on a pool, i.e., a create operation. You may see lots of this especially in the first stages, when you are learning the ZFS administration.

The best practice is to destroy a pool before reusing its components, but there are situations when you may end up with a bunch of healthy disks that someone else disposed of. They may contain disks previously in a ZFS pool, but not enough of them to import it and destroy it properly.

For such occasions, there is the -f switch, meaning force.

Train and test

Remember that creating a pool is largely one way road. You can't remove drives from it and once you decide on redundancy level, you must add new disks in the same configuration. Play with zpool and zfs commands in virtual machines. It's a low cost way of getting familiar with ZFS. Get familiar with tools that help you monitor drives: smartctl, ZED, sysstat.

CHAPTER 5

Advanced Setup

As mentioned previously, you can assign a hot spare disk to your pool. If the ZFS pool loses a disk, the spare will be automatically attached and the resilvering process will be started.

Let's consider a mirrored pool consisting of two vdevs and two drives each. Just for clarity, it will be four hard drives. They will be grouped in pairs and each pair will mirror the contents internally. If we have drives A, B, C and D, drives A and B will be one mirrored pair and drives C and D will be the second mirrored pair:

```
trochej@ubuntuzfs:~$ sudo zpool status

  pool: datapool
 state: ONLINE
  scan: none requested
config:

        NAME        STATE     READ WRITE CKSUM
        datapool    ONLINE       0     0     0
          mirror-0  ONLINE       0     0     0
            sdb     ONLINE       0     0     0
            sdc     ONLINE       0     0     0
          mirror-1  ONLINE       0     0     0
            sdd     ONLINE       0     0     0
            sde     ONLINE       0     0     0

errors: No known data errors
```

© Damian Wojsław 2017
D. Wojsław, *Introducing ZFS on Linux*, https://doi.org/10.1007/978-1-4842-3306-1_5

You add a hot spare device by running the zpool add spare command:

```
trochej@ubuntuzfs:~$ sudo zpool add datapool -f spare /dev/sdf
```

Next, confirm the disk has been added by querying the pool's status:

```
trochej@ubuntuzfs:~$ sudo zpool status datapool

  pool: datapool
 state: ONLINE
  scan: none requested
config:

    NAME          STATE     READ WRITE CKSUM
    datapool      ONLINE       0     0     0
      mirror-0    ONLINE       0     0     0
        sdb       ONLINE       0     0     0
        sdc       ONLINE       0     0     0
      mirror-1    ONLINE       0     0     0
        sdd       ONLINE       0     0     0
        sde       ONLINE       0     0     0
    spares
      sdf         AVAIL

errors: No known data errors
```

If you want to remove the spare from the pool, use the zpool remove command:

```
trochej@ubuntuzfs:~$ sudo zpool remove datapool /dev/sdf
```

You can use zpool status here too to confirm the change.

You can have a hot spare shared among more than one pool. You could create a mirrored pool that hosts very important data or data that needs to be streamed very quickly. You could then create a second pool RAIDZ that needs more space but is not that very critical (still redundant, but can only lose one disk). You can then have a hot spare assigned with both pools. The one that has failed will claim the hot spare device and then the device will not be usable for the second pool until it's freed.

Note   Using hot spares comes with one important caveat. If you plan drives in the pool in a way to minimize hardware failure impact, the hot spare may not be placed in the best way to let you keep that quality. This is true especially for shared hot spares. Many real-life installations that I have seen used spare drives. They were placed in the chassis in a way to ensure the best hardware fault resiliency in most cases. When a drive in a pool failed, the system administrator would get an alert from the monitoring system and then would replace the drive manually.

ZIL Device

ZIL stands for *ZFS Intent Log*. It is the portion of data blocks that persistently store the write cache. Normally, ZFS will allocate some blocks from the storage pool itself. However, due to the pool being busy and on a spinning disk, the performance may not be satisfying.

To better accommodate performance requirements, the ZIL (called also a SLOG) can be moved to a separate device. That device must be boot persistent, so that sudden power failure does not mean transaction data loss. In the case of RAM-based devices, they must be battery- or capacitor-powered. You can also use an SSD device.

The ZFS Admin Guide suggests that the ZIL be no less than 64 MB (it is the hard requirement for any device to be used by ZFS) and at most half of the available RAM. So for 32 GB of RAM, a 16 GB ZIL device should be used. In reality, I have rarely seen anything bigger than 32 GB, and 8 or 16 GB is the most common scenario. The reason is that this is a write buffer. Writes that would be flushed to the hard drive get grouped in the ZIL to allow for fewer physical operations and less fragmentation. Once the threshold is met, those grouped changes are written to the physical drives. Giving it a fast device, ideally a RAM device, allows for those operations to be very fast and speed writes considerably. This also allows you to divert the I/O (writing to ZIL) that would normally utilize pool bandwidth, giving the pool itself some extra performance.

To add the ZIL device, first confirm that your pool is healthy. It will also remind you which drives are part of the ZFS pool:

```
root@xubuntu:~# zpool status
 pool: data
state: ONLINE
 scan: none requested
config:

        NAME         STATE     READ WRITE CKSUM
        data         ONLINE       0     0     0
          mirror-0   ONLINE       0     0     0
            sdb      ONLINE       0     0     0
            sdc      ONLINE       0     0     0
          mirror-1   ONLINE       0     0     0
            sdd      ONLINE       0     0     0
            sde      ONLINE       0     0     0
          mirror-2   ONLINE       0     0     0
            sdf      ONLINE       0     0     0
            sdg      ONLINE       0     0     0
```

```
errors: No known data errors
```

```
 pool: rpool
state: ONLINE
 scan: none requested
config:
```

NAME	STATE	READ	WRITE	CKSUM
rpool	ONLINE	0	0	0
root_crypt	ONLINE	0	0	0

```
errors: No known data errors
```

Add the /dev/sdh and /dev/sdi drives as mirrored log devices:

```
root@xubuntu:~# zpool add -f data log mirror /dev/sdh /dev/sdi
```

While the contents of L2ARC (described in the next section) are not critical, the ZIL holds information about how your data changes on the disks. Losing ZIL will not make the ZFS file system corrupted, but it may cause some changes to be lost. Thus mirroring.

Confirm that the change is in effect by running zpool status:

```
root@xubuntu:~# zpool status data
 pool: data
state: ONLINE
 scan: none requested
config:
```

NAME	STATE	READ	WRITE	CKSUM
data	ONLINE	0	0	0
mirror-0	ONLINE	0	0	0
sdb	ONLINE	0	0	0
sdc	ONLINE	0	0	0
mirror-1	ONLINE	0	0	0

```
         sdd      ONLINE      0     0     0
         sde      ONLINE      0     0     0
     mirror-2     ONLINE      0     0     0
         sdf      ONLINE      0     0     0
         sdg      ONLINE      0     0     0
    logs
       mirror-3   ONLINE      0     0     0
         sdh      ONLINE      0     0     0
         sdi      ONLINE      0     0     0
```

errors: No known data errors

Your new log device is mirror-3.

L2ARC Device (Cache)

ZFS employs a caching technique called *Adaptive Replacement Cache*. In short it is based on the Least Recently Used (LRU) algorithm, which keeps track of access times of each cached page. It then orders them from most recently used to least recently used. The tail of the list is evicted as the new head is added.

ARC improves this algorithm by tracking pages on two lists—most recently used and most frequently used. The technical details are not as important here, but it suffice it to say, efficiency of ARC-based caches is usually much better over LRU.

ARC always exists in the memory of the operating system when the pool is imported. As a side note, if you monitor your RAM and see that most of it is being used, do not panic. There's this saying, "unused RAM is wasted RAM". Your operating system is trying to cram as much in the memory as possible, to lower the disk operations. As you know, disks are the slowest parts of the computer, even with the modern SSD drives. What you should pay attention to is how much of this utilized RAM is cache and buffers and how much is gone to running processes.

With very busy servers, it makes lots of sense to load as much data from the drives to the memory as possible, as it can speed up operations considerably.

Reading data from RAM is at least 10 times faster than reading it from hard drive. What happens, however, if you have limited memory resources and still want to cache as much as possible?

Put some SSD drives into your server and use them as L2ARC devices. L2ARCs are level-2 ARCs. Those are pages that would normally get evicted from cache, because the RAM is too small. But since there's still a very high chance of them being requested again, they may be placed in the intermediate area, on fast SSD drives.

For this reason, placing L2ARCs on mirrored SSDs makes a lot of sense.

To put /dev/sdi as a cache device into your pool, run the following:

```
root@xubuntu:~# zpool add -f data cache /dev/sdi
```

Confirm it worked:

```
root@xubuntu:~# zpool status data
 pool: data
state: ONLINE
 scan: none requested
config:
```

NAME	STATE	READ	WRITE	CKSUM
data	ONLINE	0	0	0
mirror-0	ONLINE	0	0	0
sdb	ONLINE	0	0	0
sdc	ONLINE	0	0	0
mirror-1	ONLINE	0	0	0
sdd	ONLINE	0	0	0
sde	ONLINE	0	0	0
mirror-2	ONLINE	0	0	0
sdf	ONLINE	0	0	0

```
          sdg        ONLINE        0     0     0
      logs
        sdh        ONLINE        0     0     0
      cache
        sdi        ONLINE        0     0     0

errors: No known data errors
```

Quotas and Reservations

In normal operations, every file system in a pool can take free space freely up to the full pool's capacity, until it ends. The only limitation is the other file systems also taking the space. In that regard, with ZFS you should not think in the file systems' capacities, but in the total pool space.

There are, however, situations when you need to emulate the traditional file system behavior, when they are limited to some space or guaranteed to have it for their own use.

Let's consider a traditional file system created on top of a normal disk partition. If the partition was created as 3 GB, the file system will have no less and no more than 3 GB for itself. If you mount it as, say, /var/log, then the logs in your system will have all 3 GB of space for themselves and no more than that. They will also be separate from other file systems. Thus, logs filling the /var/log directory will not make your root partition full, because they live in a separate space.

Not so with ZFS! Consider a root directory mounted on ZFS file system. Let's say the pool has 16 GB of space, total. This applies to file systems for /home, for /var, and for /var/log. After the installation of the system, suppose you're left with 11 GB of free space. Each file system can consume this space. If, for some reason, the logs go wild—maybe some application switched to debug mode and you forgot about it—they may fill this 11 GB of space, starving all other file systems. In the worst case, you won't be able to log in as root.

There are two possible actions that you can take, depending on how you wish to approach this problem: using quotas and using reservations.

Quotas are like traditional Linux quotas, except they are set against file systems and not system users. By setting up a quota, you prevent the given file system from growing beyond the set limit. So if you want /var/log to never exceed 3 GB, you will set a quota on it.

Reservations, on the other hand, are guarantees given to the file system. By setting a 3 GB reservation, you guarantee that this given file system will have at least 3 GB of space and other file systems in the pool will be prevented from claiming too much space.

To make matters a little bit more complicated, there are two versions of each: quotas and refquotas, and reservations and refreservations. The difference is quite important, as my experience taught me.

Quotas and reservations account the storage used by both the file system and its descendants. It means that this 3 GB of space will be the limit for the file system and its snapshots and clones. Refquotas, on the other hand, will only track space used by the file system itself. It opens the way for interesting scenarios, where you can separately set limits for the file system and its snapshots. But the quota comes with important twist: snapshots grow as you change the data. You must pay attention to the size of your snapshots and the rate at which they grow, or you may hit the quota before you expect it.

The same flavor distinction comes with reservations and refreservations. The reservation will guarantee space for file system and its descendants and the refreservation will only keep this space for the file system itself. Again, pay attention, as the end result of your settings may not be what you wished for nor what you expected.

Let's work through some examples based on a real-life scenario.

The server you are running has pool data. The total capacity of this pool is 30 TB. This pool will be shared by finances, engineering, and marketing. There will be also the shared space that people can use to exchange documents and silly cat pictures.

All three departments have given you the size to which their directories can grow in the future. Finances and marketing said it's going to be approximately 5 TB each and engineering said they expect it to grow up to 10 TB. Together, it gives 20 TB, leaving you with 10 TB of free space to do other things.

Now, 30 TB of space may look like a great number and for most small organizations, it probably is. On the other hand, engineering data or raw pictures and videos (in graphic studios, for example) can outgrow it quickly.

Snapshots are the subject of the next subsection, but let's just shortly introduce them here. The snapshot of a file system can be compared to the still image of file system at a given time—namely at a time of taking the snapshot. In ZFS, it can be treated like any other file system, except it's read-only. It means, looking into this file system you will see files and directories in state at exactly the moment the `zfs snapshot` command was run. No matter what happens with those files after you run this command, you can always retrieve them in the previous state from the snapshot.

The amount of space a snapshot consumes is equal to the size of changes introduced to the data. Sounds complicated, so let's demystify it. Engineering has a big CAD file size of 5 GB. It's an imported project that will be worked on. After it was copied over to the ZFS, a snapshot was taken just in case. The engineer opened the file and changed a few things. After saving it, most of the file stays the same, but some places are different. The size of those differences summed up is 300 MB. And that's the size of the snapshot. If someone deleted the file, the snapshot would grow to 5 GB, because that's the difference between the actual file system and the snapshotted moment. The mechanism behind this is explained in the next section. For now, just acknowledge this as a fact.

This space consumption by snapshots plays important role when setting up both reservations and quotas. Let's look back at the engineering department file system. The department estimated that the amount of data they will store in the file system will reach 10 TB. But they only estimated "raw" data. Files themselves, not their snapshots. Assume the daily amount of changes introduced to project files adds up to 5 GB. That is the amount of space ONE snapshot will take each day, unless it's destroyed. For simplicity, assume there's only going to be one snapshot and it will be held forever. Within a year this will amount to almost 2 TB of space taken from the pool! Now assume you create a reservation for the engineering file system and give them 10 TB. You also add a quota, 11 TB, so that they have a breathing space, but so that they won't starve other users. As assumed, their space consumption starts to near 9 TB in a year and suddenly, whole 2 TB short of target, they get an out of space error when trying to write anything. To quickly resolve the situation, they delete some old files known to be last edited a long time ago and present in several backups. Apparently, they have freed 3 TB of space, except they keep getting the out of space error. At some point they can't even delete files, because of this error!

This is the the reservation kicking in. The first part of the problem is that snapshot quietly takes space from the quota as it grows. It is only evident once you analyze space consumption using the `zpool -o space` command (explained elsewhere). But the other part of the problem, the counterintuitive out of space error when deleting things, comes from the nature of the snapshot itself. When you remove the files from the file system, those files are added to the snapshot. The only way to free this space is to destroy the snapshot using this command:

```
zfs destroy pool/engineering@snapshot
```

Now let's consider other departments. If you put a quota on them and they edit the files enough, they may soon reach their quotas due to file system snapshots. Also, most often there is more than one snapshot. It's entirely up to the policy maker, but most often there are monthly, weekly, and daily snapshots. Sometimes there are also hourly snapshots, depending on how much the data changes during the day.

Now come back to the difference between quotas and reservations and refquotas and refreservations. The first ones track whole usage, including snapshots. The latter only the file systems. For the engineering department, you could set up refquota to 11 TB and the quota to, say, 13 TB. This would open space for the snapshot to grow as files were deleted, allowing for a temporary solution. Nothing beats space utilization monitoring, though.

Quotas, reservations, refquotas, and refreservations are file system properties. It means they are set and checked using the zfs set and zfs get commands.

```
root@xubuntu:~# zfs list
NAME                USED  AVAIL  REFER  MOUNTPOINT
data                179K  2.86G    19K  /data
data/engineering     19K  2.86G    19K  /data/engineering
```

To check the current values of quota, refquota, reservation, and refreservation on the data/engineering file system, run the following:

```
root@xubuntu:~# zfs get quota,refquota,reservation,refreservation
data/engineering
NAME                PROPERTY        VALUE     SOURCE
data/engineering    quota           none      default
data/engineering    refquota        none      default
data/engineering    reservation     none      default
data/engineering    refreservation  none      default
```

They are not set by default, as you can see. Since my test pool is much smaller than the considered scenario, let's set the reservation to 1 GB and the quota to 1.5 GB with a bit lower refquota and refreservation:

```
root@xubuntu:~# zfs set quota=1.5G data/engineering
root@xubuntu:~# zfs set refquota=1G data/engineering
root@xubuntu:~# zfs set reservation=800M data/engineering
```

```
root@xubuntu:~# zfs get quota,refquota,reservation data/
engineering
NAME               PROPERTY     VALUE    SOURCE
data/engineering   quota        1.50G    local
data/engineering   refquota     1G       local
data/engineering   reservation  800M     local
```

Snapshots and Clones

Here we come to discuss snapshots and clones, two powerful features of ZFS. They were already discussed a bit earlier, so here is the time for detailed explanation.

As explained, snapshots are a way of "freezing" the file system contents at a given time. Due to the Copy on Write nature of ZFS, creating snapshots is fast (takes usually a fraction of a second) and takes very little processing power. It is thus common to create snapshots as a basis for long-running jobs that require contents to be static, like for example backup jobs. Running a backup job from a large file system may archive files at different times. Running it off a snapshot guarantees that all files will be captured at the same exact time, even if the backup is running for hours. Additionally, if backed up files consist of state files of an application that needs to be shut down for the duration of the backup process, the down time of this application can be reduced to mere fractions of a second.

One additional property of a snapshot is the ability to roll back the current file system to the snapshot. It means that the administrator can rewind all the files to the moment of snapshot creation.

ZFS writes changed blocks in a new location in the pool. Thus it leaves old blocks untouched unless the pool is filled and the old space needs to be reclaimed. Due to this, snapshots are automatically mounted into the .zfs/snapshot subdirectory of a snapped file system. As an example,

71

for the data/documents ZFS file system, if there is a snapshot data/documents@initial, the contents of this snapshot can be accessed by looking into /data/documents/.zfs/snapshot/initial.

Snapshot contents can be accessed either looking into the directory above or by running a rollback command, which effectively rewinds the file system to the moment of snapshot creation. The process is very fast. It only takes as much time as updating some metadata. The administrator needs to exercise some caution though—once rolled back the file system can't be fast forwarded to its current state.

There are situations where a read-only snapshot is not enough and it might be useful to be able to use it as a normal file system. ZFS has such a feature and it's called a *clone*. A clone is a read-write copy of a snapshot. Initially, clone and snapshot refer the same set of bytes, thus the clone does not consume any disk space. When changes are introduced to the clone's contents, it starts to take space.

A clone and a snapshot it was created from are related in a parent-child manner. As long as clone is in use, the snapshot cannot be destroyed.

Why are snapshots useful? They can guard against files corruptions by faulty software or accidental deletions. They can also provide a means of looking into the file before some edit. They can be used as a snapshot of file system prepared to be backed up.

Why are clones useful? One interesting use of clones is to create one before important updates of an operating system. Long known in the world of illumos and FreeBSD, boot environments are root file system clones that can be booted into. This allows for a quick reboot to a known working operating system after a broken upgrade. They have been also used as means of cloning containers and virtual machines. The uses are limited by imagination.

Now, after this introduction, onto the usage itself.

ZFS ACLs

Linux is an operating system from the Unix tradition. The Unix operating systems are multi-user systems, allowing many users to operate the same computer. This brought a standard model of file and directory permissions control. In this model, there are three types of actions and three types of actors. The actions are read, write, and execute and the actors are owner, group, and all others. Both can be combined, giving a simple, yet quite effective way of restricting and granting access to certain directories and files in Linux. This model is known as *discretionary access control* (DAC).

DAC allows for flexible control of who can utilize certain system areas and how. However, the more users and the more complex organizational structure, the more difficult it is to express them using the DAC model. At some point, it becomes impossible. Thus, a new way of representing access control method was invented.

Linux adopted POSIX ACLs. ACL means access control list and is exactly that: a list of access controlling entries that can create much more fine-grained policies about who can read, write, or execute a given file and how they do so.

ZFS on its default operating system—illumos—supports separate sets of ACLs, conformant with NTFS ACLs. They are set and listed by extended ls and chmod commands. Unfortunately, those commands are different from their Linux counterparts and thus on Linux, standard ZFS ACLs are unsupported. This means that if the system administrator wants to go beyond the DAC model, they have to utilize POSIX ACLs and standard commands: setfacl for specifying the list and getfacl for listing it. The upside is that every other major Linux file system uses those commands, thus you only need to learn once. The downside is, if you ever have a pool imported from illumos or FreeBSD, ACLs may go missing.

DAC Model

Before I explain POSIX ACLs, I first need to explain the DAC model using a simple scenario.

Assume there's a server that has three users: Alice, John, and Mikey. Alice is a project manager, John is a programmer, and Mikey works in accounting. There are three directories on the server that are accessible to users:

- Code: it's contains what it says: the source code for the project that Alice manages and John codes. Company policy says that both Alice and John should be able to access the contents of this directory, but only John can add new files or edit existing ones. Mikey should not see the contents of this directory.

- Documents: This directory contains typical project documentation. Architecture analysis, project overview, milestones, customer signoffs, etc. Company policy says Mikey and John should be able to read these files, but not edit them, and Alice should be able to both read and edit files.

- Accounts: This directory contains financial data: time accounting from John and Alice, invoices for customers and from contractors related to the project, budget, etc. Mikey has full control over these files. Alice should be able to read them all, but edit only some, and John should not be able to do either.

This, obviously, doesn't reflect a real-life programming project, but it is sufficient for our purposes. Traditional DAC model tools that we have are:

- System users and groups

- Directory and file access controls

- Each directory and file has an owner (system user) and a group (system group that also owns the directory or the file)

Having those three allows us to do quite a lot regarding management in this small scenario.

Let's start by creating ZFS file systems for each of these directories. Assume the directory is called data. For better data accessibility, the pool is mirrored.

```
$ sudo zpool create data mirror /dev/sdb1 /dev/sdc1
```

Now that we have a pool, we create file systems for the three directories:

```
$ sudo zfs create data/Code
$ sudo zfs create data/Documents
$ sudo zfs create data/Accounts
```

Assume that system users for Alice, John, and Mickey already exist and their logins are, surprise, alice, john, mickey, accordingly. Additionally, three groups have been defined: projmgmt for project managers, devel for developers, and accnt for accounting. Before we set up permissions, let's create a table that will exactly describe who should be able to do what. It's a good practice when setting up file server structure to prepare such a matrix. It helps tidy up and visualize things.

Access control uses three letters to denote the rights assigned to user or group:

- r – read

- w – write

- x – execute. This bit set on directory means that the user or group can see its contents. You actually can't execute a directory. To differentiate between execute and access, x is used for the first and X is used for the latter.

Table 1-1 quickly makes it obvious that groups have the same rights as the users that belong to them. It may then seem like overkill to duplicate access rights for both. At this point in time it certainly is, but we should always plan for the future. It's not a lot of work to manage both group and user rights and each directory needs to have its owning group specified anyway. And, if in the future, any of those groups gains another user, giving them privileges will be as easy as adding them to the group to which they should belong.

Table 1-1. *Project Directories, Users, Groups, and Access Rights*

User/Group/Directory	Alice	John	Mickey	projmgmt	devel	accnt
Code	rX	rwX	---	rX	rwX	---
Documents	rwX	rX	rX	rwX	rX	rX
Accounts	rX	---	rwX	rX	---	rwX

This doesn't account for separate users who will run backup daemons and should at least be able to read all directories to back up their contents and maybe write, to recreate them if need be. In this example, backups can be done by snapshotting the directories and using zfs send|zfs recv to store them on a separate pool, where special daemons can put them on tapes.

For now, the following commands will be sufficient, if we want to apply just the user and owner's group rights.

```
$ sudo chown -R alice:projmgmt data/Documents
$ sudo chown -R john:devel data/Code
$ sudo chown -R mickey:accnt data/Accounts
$ sudo chmod -R =0770 data/Documents
$ sudo chmod -R =0770 data/Code
$ sudo chmod -R =0770 data/Accounts
```

The =0770 is an octal mode of setting permissions. The equals sign means we want to set permissions exactly as in the string, the leading zero is of no interest at this point, and the second, third, and fourth digits are the permissions for owner, owning group, and all others accordingly. The permissions set are represented by numbers and their sum: 4 – read, 2 – write, and 1 – execute. Any sum of those will create a unique number: 5 means read and execute, 6 means read and write, and 7 means all of above. The octal mode is a very convenient way of setting all bits at once. If we wanted to use named mode, user, group, or others, we would have to run this command once for each:

```
$ sudo chmod -R ug=rwX data/Documents
$ sudo chmod -R o-rwX data/Documents
```

This command creates the set of permissions reflected in Table 1-2.

Table 1-2. *Project Directories, Users, Groups, and Access Rights After First Commands*

User/Group/Directory	Alice	John	Mickey	projmgmt	devel	accnt
Code	---	rwX	---	---	rwX	---
Documents	rwX	---	---	rwX	---	---
Accounts	---	---	rwX	---	---	rwX

Obviously, this is not the set we wanted to achieve. One way to tackle it is to change the owning group to the one that needs read access:

```
$ sudo chown -R john:projmgmt data/Code
$ sudo chmod -R =0750 data/Code
```

This gives Alice access to read the Code directory; however, it doesn't solve the problem of another person joining the project management or accounting group. Let's assume that Susan joins the PM team and needs to have the same set of permissions as Alice. With the current model, this is impossible to achieve. This is where ACLs come in to play.

ACLs Explained

ZFS doesn't allow the use of Linux ACLs (or rather POSIX ACLs) out of the box. It needs to be told to do this. The command to run is:

```
$ sudo zfs set acltype=posixacl data
```

This command turns on POSIX ACLs for a given file system. This property is by default inherited by all the child file systems, so if it's set on a root of ZFS, it will be propagated all the way down. You can verify it by running the zfs get command:

```
$ sudo zfs get acltype data
NAME   PROPERTY   VALUE     SOURCE
lxd    acltype    posixacl  local
```

How do ACLs help solve the problem above? It's simple. They allow developers to store more than those three DAC entries used previously. It is possible to have a separate permission set per additional user or group. There are two tools used to administer ACLs: setfactl and getfacl.

```
$ setfacl -m g:projmgmt:r /data/Code
$ setfacl -m g:devel:r /data/Documents
```

```
$ setfacl -m g:accnt:r /data/Documents
$ setfacl -m g:projmgmt:r /data/Accounts
```

Remember that ACL commands operate on directories, not on ZFS file systems!

These commands will give additional groups exact rights, as in Table 1-1, just as expected. We can confirm that by running getfacl for each directory, as follows:

```
$ getfacl /data/Documents
getfacl: Removing leading '/' from absolute path names
# file: data/Documents
# owner: alice
# group: projmgmt
user::rwx
group::rwx
group:devel:r--
group:accnt:r--
mask::r-x
other::r-x
```

The syntax for setfacl mode is as follows:

```
setfacl -mode:user|group:permissions directory[/file]
```

The setfacl command works in two modes: add ACL entry or remove ACL entry. Use the -m and -x switches accordingly. In the previous example, the -m switch was used to add an ACL list entry to a specific group. To remove an entry, you need to run the command with the -x switch:

```
$ setfacl -x g:devel /data/Documents
```

This will remove all ACL entries for the devel group added to the /data/Documents directory.

Replacing Drive

There are many scenarios in which you may need to replace drives. Most common is drive failure. Either your monitoring systems warned you about upcoming drive failure or the drive has failed. Either way you need to add new drive to the pool and remove old one.

There is another reason for replacing a drive. This is one of methods, slow and cumbersome, of growing ZFS pool without adding drives - by replacing old ones, one by one, with larger disks.

Consider first scenario. You pool is reported as healthy in `zpool` status output, but you know one of drives is going to fail soon. Assume that in pool printed below drive to fail is `sdb`.

```
NAME        STATE    READ   WRITE   CKSUM
tank        ONLINE    0       0       0
  mirror-0  ONLINE    0       0       0
    sdb     ONLINE    0       0       0
    sdc     ONLINE    0       0       0
```

Assume you have added drive, `sdd`, to the system. You can either run `zpool` replace command:

```
sudo zpool replace tank sdb sdd
```

which will attach `sdd` to `sdb` forming a mirror for short time and then remove `sdb` from the pool. Or you can do it in two steps, first attach `sdd` to `sdb` manually, wait until resilver is complete and then remove `sdb` yourself:

```
sudo zpool attach tank sdb sdd

sudo zpool status
  pool: tank
 state: ONLINE
```

```
scan: resilvered 114K in 0h0m with 0 errors on Tue Nov 7
   21:35:58 2017
config:
```

NAME	STATE	READ	WRITE	CKSUM
tank	ONLINE	0	0	0
mirror-0	ONLINE	0	0	0
sdb	ONLINE	0	0	0
sdc	ONLINE	0	0	0
sdd	ONLINE	0	0	0

You can see this has effectively turned mirror-0 into three way mirror. Monitor the resilver process and when it's done issue:

```
sudo zpool detach tank sdb
```

which will remove sdb device from your pool.

In case when the drive has already failed steps are similar as above, except you will see

NAME	STATE	READ	WRITE	CKSUM
tank	DEGRADED	0	0	0
mirror-0	DEGRADED	0	0	0
sdb	UNAVAIL	0	0	0
sdc	ONLINE	0	0	0

Follow the steps are previously:

```
sudo zpool replace tank sdb sdd
```

This will replace the failed drive with new one.

Growing the pool without adding new drives means replacing every disk in a pool with new one, bigger. Assume you would want to make the pool tank something bigger than current 2 GB:

```
sudo zpool list
NAME SIZE  ALLOC FREE   EXPANDSZ FRAG CAP DEDUP HEALTH ALTROOT
tank 1.98G 152K  1.98G  -        0%   0%  1.00x ONLINE -
```

The steps would mean:

1. Add new drives into the chassis. They have to be the same geometry and size.

2. Attach new, bigger drive to the mirror and wait until it finishes the resilver process.

3. Remove old drive.

4. Attach next bigger drive. Wait for resilver, remove.

Instead of attaching and removing you can run replace command. It will do all the steps above for you:

```
sudo zpool replace tank sdb sdd
```

If you have pool built of more than one vdev, you can run replace command for each vdev. This will speed things a bit.

CHAPTER 6

Sharing

Once you have your storage set up and configured the way you like, it is time to start using it. One way is to use the space used by local programs running on the same server as the ZFS pool. This is particularly useful if you intend to host applications such as mail, web pages, or applications (internal or external CRMs, perhaps). On the other hand, you may need to provide common disk space to client machines, for example, workstations that will store data on the server or share documents for editing.

Your choice of connection method, known as the *sharing protocol*, is dictated by the way you are going to use the space.

Sharing Protocols

As with any storage array, there are two basic ways you can share the disk space: as a character device or a block device. The difference is in how the device is used and relays to the basic two groups of devices in Linux—character devices and block devices. For our needs, the difference can be summed this way: a character device will be, in our context, a file system that can be mounted and used directly to store and retrieve files. A block device is a pseudo-device, a file system, which can only be used by treating it as a hard drive itself.

© Damian Wojsław 2017
D. Wojsław, *Introducing ZFS on Linux*, https://doi.org/10.1007/978-1-4842-3306-1_6

Given the DYI small storage array, character devices would be one of two popular network file system sharing protocols—NFS or CIFS. Block devices will most likely be the iSCSI protocol. While you may decide to use FC or FCoE protocols, I am not going to cover them here.

The original ZFS implementation allows for quick sharing through NFS and CIFS protocols. The commands are tightly bound to ZFS itself and are represented at a file system or a zvol property. Currently, at the time this guide is written, the native ZFS share commands don't work with the Linux platform or work unreliably. As with ACLs, you need to use Linux native tools—iSCSAadm, samba, and NFS servers—to provide this functionality.

Note   Please be aware that describing complex NFS, Samba, or iSCSI configurations warrant separate books on their own. Those are out of the scope of this simple guide. There are a number of books and a very large number of tutorials for each of them available on the Internet, in case you need to work on something more complex.

NFS: Linux Server

NFS is a flexible and proven network storage sharing protocol. It was conceived by Sun Microsystems in 1984. It is a networked file system for distributed environments. One quite common use in the Unix world is to host users' home directories on the NFS server and automount them on given machines when the user logs in. Thus the same home is always available in one, central location (which is easy for backup and restore), but reachable on any workstation that's configured to use the NFS server.

NFS is quite common in the Unix and Linux world and is a standard way of sharing disk space between server and client machines. On the other hand, if you need to use the disk space from Windows systems, it will be beneficial to configure a SAMBA server.

There are two dominant versions of the NFS protocol: version 3 and version 4. If possible, use version 4, as it is now well supported by major Linux distributions. Version 4 adds many performance and security improvements and made strong security mandatory. I present the steps to install and configure NFSv4. The packages are the same, but some configurations differ. Before you start using NFS on the server and client machines, there are some steps you need to take. First, the packages need to be installed.

Installing Packages on Ubuntu

To install and configure NFS server on Ubuntu, run the following:

```
trochej@ubuntu:~$ sudo apt-get install nfs-kernel-server
[sudo] password for trochej:
Reading package lists... Done
Building dependency tree
Reading state information... Done
The following additional packages will be installed:
 keyutils libnfsidmap2 libpython-stdlib libpython2.7-minimal
 libpython2.7-stdlib
 libtirpc1 nfs-common python python-minimal python2.7
 python2.7-minimal rpcbind
Suggested packages:
 watchdog python-doc python-tk python2.7-doc binutils binfmt-
 support
The following NEW packages will be installed:
 keyutils libnfsidmap2 libpython-stdlib libpython2.7-minimal
 libpython2.7-stdlib
 libtirpc1 nfs-common nfs-kernel-server python python-minimal
 python2.7
 python2.7-minimal rpcbind
```

```
0 upgraded, 13 newly installed, 0 to remove and 96 not upgraded.
Need to get 4,383 kB of archives.
After this operation, 18.5 MB of additional disk space will be used.
Do you want to continue? [Y/n]
```

After you press Y and confirm with Enter, the system will print a list of the packages it installs. Your output may vary from what's shown here, depending on what you have already installed. Assume that the pool tank and file system export exist on the server:

trochej@ubuntu:~$ sudo zfs list
```
NAME            USED  AVAIL  REFER  MOUNTPOINT
tank            80K   1.92G   19K   /tank
tank/export     19K   1.92G   19K   /tank/export
```

Edit the /etc/exports file (it is a listing of directories exported via NFS protocol and various options applied to them) and add this line:

```
/tank/export      192.168.0.0/24(rw,fsid=0,sync)
```

This will make the /tank/export file system available to all hosts in the 192.168.0.0 network.

The fsid=0 option tells the NFS server that the directory is a root for other file systems. The rw option sets the file system to read-write. Sync tells the server to only confirm the write when the buffer has been committed to the physical media.

To make this export available over the network, the kernel server needs to be restarted:

```
sudo systemctl restart nfs-kernel-server
```

The last thing to make sure of is to change permissions on the exported file system so that the remote server can write to it:

trochej@ubuntu:~$ `sudo chmod -R a+rwX /tank/`

You can confirm the export by running the `exportfs` command:

trochej@ubuntu:~$ `sudo exportfs`
```
/tank/export    192.168.0.0/24
```

Installing NFS Client on Ubuntu

To install and configure NFS client on a Ubuntu machine, run:

```
sudo apt-get install nfs-common
```

Then test the mount by running this:

```
sudo mount -t nfs4 -o proto=tcp,port=2049 192.168.0.9:/ /mnt
```

This will tell the `mount` command to mount a remote file system running on a 192.168.0.9 server in the /mnt directory. Making it persistent across reboots requires you to add this line to the /etc/fstab file:

```
192.168.0.9:/   /mnt    nfs4    _netdev,auto  0  0
```

From now on, your ZFS pool is exported and available remotely to the client machine.

Installing Packages on CentOS

To achieve the same on CentOS, run the following:

```
[root@centos ~]# yum install nfs-utils
```

Change permissions on the directory:

```
[root@centos ~]# chmod -R a+rwX /tank/export
```

Next, add the appropriate entry to /etc/exports:

```
[root@centos ~]# cat /etc/exports
/tank/export 192.168.0.0/24(rw,fsid=0,sync)
```

Finally, restart the NFS server:

```
[root@centos ~]# systemctl restart nfs-server
```

Mounting it on the client is similar.

```
[root@centos ~]# yum install nfs-utils
[root@centos ~]# mount -t nfs4 -o proto=tcp,port=2049
192.168.0.9:/ /mnt
```

As with Ubuntu, to make the mount automatic on every system boot, add the following line to your /etc/fstab file:

```
192.168.0.9:/   /mnt    nfs4    _netdev,auto  0  0
```

This setup is very crude. No security has been applied and absolutely no external user authentication method is in use. Usually, in a production environment, you will want to use some kind of central user database, such as LDAP or Active Directory.

SAMBA

Configuring SAMBA is more complex even for simplest setups. It requires editing appropriate configuration file. In Ubuntu it is /etc/samba/smb.conf

Below I paste absolutely smallest smb.conf file I could figure:

```
[global]
  workgroup = WORKGROUP
  server string = %h server (Samba, Ubuntu)
  dns proxy = no
  server role = standalone server
  passdb backend = tdbsam
```

```
[shared]
  comment = Shared ZFS Pool
  path = /tank/
  browseable = yes
  read only = no
  guest ok = yes
  writeable = yes
```

The configuration above is absolutely unfit in real world. It offers no way of sensible logging, no security, no password synchronization. Just anonymous access to exported pool. But it serves a purpose of test.

Mounting this on Linux machine is simple:

```
sudo mount -t cifs //CIFSSERVER/shared /mnt
```

Where CIFSSERVER is the IP address or resolvable network name of the SAMBA server. Note that once users get involved the line above will have to change.

Mounting this share in Windows machine is as simple as opening Explorer Window, navigating to CIFSSERVER in the network and opening the share. Done.

As with NFS, you will most probably want to involve some additional directory services, kinds of LDAP. You absolutely must not use anonymous shares in real world. Just don't.

As with NFS, the material to learn is a book on its own and there is abundance of sources on the internet.

Other Sharing Protocols

ZFS allows for even more ways of sharing. Of special interest might be iSCSI or Fiber Channel. SCSI (Small Computer System Interface) is the de facto standard for connecting hard drives to the server in enterprise setups. Currently, the Serial Attached SCSI (commonly known as SAS) is the technology to use. While the protocol was designed to connect many other peripherals to the computer, in the server rooms it's dominant for connecting drives.

As noted, ZFS can create file systems that act like directories. You can create block devices, called ZVOLs. They are treated like normal hard drives that can be partitioned and formatted. They can also be exported as physical drives by means of the iSCSI protocol.

iSCSI is an implementation of the SCSI protocol over TCP/IP networks. It allows you to carry out SCSI commands to storage devices over the network, as if they were directly attached to the system.

Two important SCSI (and hence iSCSI) terms are *initiator* and *target*. The target is the storage resource; in this scenario, it's available over the network. The *initiator* is the iSCSI client. To utilize the storage initiator, you must log in to the target and initiate a session. If configured like this, it can force authentication of client to the server.

Using the iSCSI protocol on Linux platform is pretty easy. First you need to create ZVOLs and export each of them as a LUN (logical unit).

First, let's create ZVOLs to be used as virtual drives. Those will be vol01, vol02, vol03, and vol04 living in the data pool.

```
sudo zfs create -V 5gb data/vol01
sudo zfs create -V 5gb data/vol02
sudo zfs create -V 5gb data/vol03
sudo zfs create -V 5gb data/vol04
```

The next step is to create four LUNs that will present ZVOLs to the client machines:

```
sudo tgtadm --lld iscsi --op new --mode target --tid 1 -
T iqn.2016.temp:storage.lun01
sudo tgtadm --lld iscsi --op new --mode target --tid 2 -
T iqn.2016.temp:storage.lun02
```

```
sudo tgtadm --lld iscsi --op new --mode target --tid 3 -
T iqn.2016.temp:storage.lun03
sudo tgtadm --lld iscsi --op new --mode target --tid 4 -
T iqn.2016.temp:storage.lun04
```

Once you're done, the ZVOLs must be exported as LUNs via the
previously configured targets:

```
sudo tgtadm --lld iscsi --op new --mode logicalunit --tid 1
--lun 1 -b /dev/zvol/data/vol01
sudo tgtadm --lld iscsi --op new --mode logicalunit --tid 2
--lun 1 -b /dev/zvol/data/vol02
sudo tgtadm --lld iscsi --op new --mode logicalunit --tid 3
--lun 1 -b /dev/zvol/data/vol03
sudo tgtadm --lld iscsi --op new --mode logicalunit --tid 4
--lun 1 -b /dev/zvol/data/vol04
sudo tgtadm --lld iscsi --mode target --op bind --tid 1 -I ALL
sudo tgtadm --lld iscsi --mode target --op bind --tid 2 -I ALL
sudo tgtadm --lld iscsi --mode target --op bind --tid 3 -I ALL
sudo tgtadm --lld iscsi --mode target --op bind --tid 4 -I ALL
sudo tgt-admin --dump | sudo tee /etc/tgt/targets.conf
```

You can confirm the configuration by running the tgadm command.
The following output has been cut for brevity:

```
trochej@hypervizor:~$ sudo tgtadm --mode tgt --op show
Target 1: iqn.2016.temp:storage.lun01
        System information:
                Driver: iscsi
                State: ready
        I_T nexus information:
        LUN information:
                LUN: 0
```

Type: controller
SCSI ID: IET   00010000
SCSI SN: beaf10
Size: 0 MB, Block size: 1
Online: Yes
Removable media: No
Prevent removal: No
Readonly: No
SWP: No
Thin-provisioning: No
Backing store type: null
Backing store path: None
Backing store flags:
LUN: 1

Type: disk
SCSI ID: IET   00010001
SCSI SN: beaf11
Size: 5369 MB, Block size: 512
Online: Yes
Removable media: No
Prevent removal: No
Readonly: No
SWP: No
Thin-provisioning: No
Backing store type: rdwr
Backing store path: /dev/zvol/data/vol01
Backing store flags:
Account information:
ACL information:
ALL

Connecting initiators to targets is done by using the `iscsiadm` command:

```
iscsiadm -m discovery -t sendtargets -p 192.168.0.9
192.168.0.9:3260,1 iqn.2016.temp:storage.lun01:target1
```

This command will print targets configured on the server. To start using them, the client machine needs to log in and start the session:

```
iscsiadm -m node -T iqn.2016.temp:storage.lun01:target1 --login
```

You can confirm the disks appearing in the system by grepping:

```
root@madtower:/home/trochej# dmesg | grep "Attached SCSI disk"
[...]
        [ 3772.041014] sd 5:0:0:1: [sdc] Attached SCSI disk
        [ 3772.041016] sd 4:0:0:1: [sdb] Attached SCSI disk
        [ 3772.047183] sd 6:0:0:1: [sde] Attached SCSI disk
        [ 3772.050148] sd 7:0:0:1: [sdd] Attached SCSI disk
[...]
```

Having four LUNs available in the system, the only step remaining is to use them as you would use any other physical drive. You can create an LVM pool on them or even on another ZFS pool:

```
root@madtower:/home/trochej# zpool create -f datapool mirror /
dev/sdb /dev/sdc mirror /dev/sdd /dev/sde
root@madtower:/home/trochej# zpool list
NAME        SIZE  ALLOC   FREE  EXPANDSZ   FRAG   CAP  DEDUP
HEALTH   ALTROOT
datapool  9.94G  68.5K  9.94G         -     0%    0%  1.00x
ONLINE   -
rpool      444G   133G   311G         -    29%   29%  1.00x
ONLINE   -
```

```
root@madtower:/home/trochej# zpool status datapool
  pool: datapool
 state: ONLINE
  scan: none requested
config:

                NAME       STATE     READ WRITE CKSUM
                datapool   ONLINE       0     0     0
                  mirror-0 ONLINE       0     0     0
                    sdb    ONLINE       0     0     0
                    sdc    ONLINE       0     0     0
                  mirror-1 ONLINE       0     0     0
                    sdd    ONLINE       0     0     0
                    sde    ONLINE       0     0     0

errors: No known data errors
```

You have a lot of choices when exporting your pool for use by client machines. I've only covered three of them as they seem to be most popular.

CHAPTER 7

Space Accounting

With such a rich feature set, including clones, snapshots, and compression all relying on file system organization, space monitoring needs to be done differently from the traditional Linux file systems. The usual *df _-h_* \ command familiar to every Linux server administrator is no longer sufficient and may even be misleading.

Using New Commands

With ZFS, you need to learn two new commands and understand their arguments and output to keep track of your free space—*sudo zpool list* and *sudo zfs list*. On my home workstation, these commands produce the following output.

```
trochej@madchamber:~$ sudo zpool list

NAME    SIZE  ALLOC   FREE  EXPANDSZ   FRAG   CAP  DEDUP
HEALTH   ALTROOT
data  2,72T   147G  2,58T         -     3%    5%  1.00x
ONLINE   -

trochej@madchamber:~$ sudo zfs list

NAME          USED  AVAIL  REFER  MOUNTPOINT
data          147G  2,53T    96K  /data
data/datafs   147G  2,53T   147G  /mnt/data
```

© Damian Wojsław 2017
D. Wojsław, *Introducing ZFS on Linux*, https://doi.org/10.1007/978-1-4842-3306-1_7

This list is not complete because it omits snapshots by default. Remember, snapshots consume space increasingly with time, as data changes on the snapshotted system. In my experience a common issue raised by new ZFS storage operators is that they are unable to delete data due to lack of space. They are usually baffled by the fact that deleting data won't increase the available space, and that consumed space in a ZFS list won't add up to the total space available in the pool.

Output Terminology

Let's look at the columns in the output and learn what they mean to the operator:

- AVAIL means available. Total available space in the file system.

- USED means used. Total used space in the file system.

- USEDSNAP means used by snapshots. The disk space used by snapshots of the dataset. This space is freed once all snapshots of the dataset are destroyed. Since multiple snapshots can reference the same blocks, this amount may not be equal to the sum of all snapshots' used space.

- USEDDS means used by dataset. The disk space used by the dataset itself. This disk space is freed if all snapshots and refreservations of this dataset were destroyed, thus destroying the dataset itself.

- USEDREFRESERV means used by refreservation. The disk space used by a refreservation set on the dataset. This space is freed once refreservation is removed.

- USEDCHILD means used by children. The disk space used by children of the dataset. This space is freed after destroying the children of a given dataset.

To calculate the USED property by hand, follow this equation: USED = USEDCHILD + USEDDS + USEDREFRESERV + USEDSNAP.

What's Consuming My Pool Space?

It is sometimes a bit difficult to understand what consumes your pool space. I will demonstrate ways to figure it out using some examples, but nothing beats experience. Create a pool, fill it with data, run snapshots, and delete and create reservations. All the while, observe *zfs list_ -t all -o snapshot_* and *zfs list _-t all_* to better understand the space accounting.

Diagnosing the Problem

Let's consider a situation in which you have a 3 TB pool.

```
sudo zpool create datapool mirror /dev/sdb /dev/sdc
sudo zfs create datapool/data
```

After successful import of 2 TB of backed up data, you decide to create a snapshot so that users mistakenly deleting data won't require you to rerun the backup restore.

```
sudo zfs snapshot datapool/data@after-backup-restore
```

Note that running this snapshot is instantaneous and takes no disk space initially.

Perhaps, as sometimes can happen, just after you run the snapshot, a user with very wide access rights accidentally deletes a whole 2 TB of data. But, the delete job stops short of 1 TB with information, reporting that it cannot delete more due to the lack of space. How is that possible? The answer is: the snapshot. Let's first observe the file system on my workstation:

```
trochej@madchamber:~$ sudo zfs list
```

```
NAME            USED   AVAIL   REFER   MOUNTPOINT
data            134G   2,55T     96K   /data
data/datafs     134G   2,55T    134G   /mnt/data
```

Now, we create a snapshot there:

```
trochej@madchamber:~$ sudo zfs snapshot data/datafs@testsnapshot
```

```
trochej@madchamber:~$ sudo zfs list -t all
```

```
NAME                        USED   AVAIL   REFER   MOUNTPOINT
data                        134G   2,55T     96K   /data
data/datafs                 134G   2,55T    134G   /mnt/data
data/datafs@testsnapshot       0       -    134G   -
```

Now we upload a CentOS 7 GB ISO file to _/mnt/data_:

```
trochej@madchamber:~$ sudo zfs list -t all
```

```
NAME                        USED   AVAIL   REFER   MOUNTPOINT
data                        141G   2,54T     96K   /data
data/datafs                 141G   2,54T    134G   /mnt/data
data/datafs@testsnapshot   7,14G       -    134G   -
```

Notice that the snapshot size has increased up to the newly introduced data. Let's now delete the whole directory containing the archived ISOs:

```
trochej@madchamber:~$ sudo zfs list -t all
```

```
NAME                        USED   AVAIL   REFER   MOUNTPOINT
data                        141G   2,54T     96K   /data
data/datafs                 141G   2,54T    109G   /mnt/data
data/datafs@testsnapshot   32,0G       -    134G   -
```

What you will see is that while the REFER size for the data/datafs ZFS file system has shrunk, the overall USED stays the same and the snapshot size has increased to 32 GB. For comparison, let's look at the *df _-h_ * command (I removed the non-ZFS file systems from the output for clarity):

```
trochej@madchamber:~$ df -h

Filesystem      Size  Used Avail Use% Mounted on
data            2,6T  128K  2,6T   1% /data
data/datafs     2,7T  109G  2,6T   5% /mnt/data
```

Let's now remove some more data from datafs, just to increase the size of the snapshot:

```
trochej@madchamber:~$ sudo zfs list -t all

NAME                         USED  AVAIL  REFER  MOUNTPOINT
data                         141G  2,54T    96K  /data
data/datafs                  141G  2,54T  23,3G  /mnt/data
data/datafs@testsnapshot     117G      -   134G  -

trochej@madchamber:~$ df -h

Filesystem      Size  Used Avail Use% Mounted on
data            2,6T  128K  2,6T   1% /data
data/datafs     2,6T   24G  2,6T   1% /mnt/data
```

As you may notice, there is not much to be gleaned from the du command. It more or less tracks the space usage, but it tells us nothing about the pattern. The zfs list, on the other hand, tells us quite a lot. By this output alone, you can see that while your file system used space has shrunk, the overall used stays the same; it has just moved into another dataset's location.

The *zfs* command can provide you with an even deeper understanding of how the space is distributed among your data. And while it's not very interesting in the case of the small experiment I've been running so far, I'll provide you with more complicated examples in just a moment. First, however, let's check out another option for *zfs list*:

```
trochej@madchamber:~$ sudo zfs list -t all -o space
```

NAME		AVAIL	USED	USEDSNAP	USEDDS
USEDREFRESERV	USEDCHILD				
data		2,54T	141G	0	96K
0	141G				
data/datafs		2,54T	141G	117G	23,3G
0	0				
data/datafs@testsnapshot		-	117G	-	-
-	-				

Note   A more detailed explanation of -o space follows in the next section.

It should now be pretty clear where the issue with data deletion came from. Since the 3 TB pool is capable of keeping more or less the same amount of data (modulo data compression), introducing the deletion of 2 TB of data on a file system that already holds 2 TB results in pool space running out, since the pool needs to add data to the snapshot as the user keeps removing it.

More Advanced Examples

The previous example is pretty simple. Not much is happening on this pool and not many additional features were used. Let's create a sample ZFS pool using file storage (files emulating real block devices) and we will play with a few scenarios to see how setting up various ZFS properties affects available space and the zfs -o space output.

The *zfs _-o space_* output is not very informative and interesting in the previous example, so let's consider the following configurations:

- A pool named datapool with RAIDZ2 redundancy.

- Five file systems, two of which have regular snapshots taken each hour and retained for two weeks. Every Saturday a snapshot is taken, and it is retained for a month.

- Two of the file systems have a quota set.

- One file system has set reservations.

- One zvol is created.

Let's put this configuration into print:

```
trochej@ubuntuzfs:~$ sudo zpool list

NAME        SIZE  ALLOC   FREE  EXPANDSZ   FRAG   CAP  DEDUP
HEALTH   ALTROOT
datapool  23.8G  5.37G  18.4G         -    14%   22%  1.00x
ONLINE   -
```

So the pool says that there is more than 18 GB of space free in the pool. Let's look closer:

```
trochej@ubuntuzfs:~$ sudo zfs list

NAME              USED  AVAIL  REFER  MOUNTPOINT
datapool         13.2G  2.41G  34.0K  /datapool
datapool/first   3.58G  6.83G  3.58G  /datapool/first
```

```
datapool/five      50.0K   2.41G   32.0K   /datapool/five
datapool/fourth    50.0K   2.41G   32.0K   /datapool/fourth
datapool/second    50.0K   2.41G   32.0K   /datapool/second
datapool/third     50.0K   2.41G   32.0K   /datapool/third
datapool/vol01     5.16G   7.57G   16.0K   -
```

But not exactly. Shouldn't the AVAIL number be the same as FREE in the *zpool list* output? ZFS file systems can grow up to the pool's capacity. Let's list *all* datasets:

```
trochej@ubuntuzfs:~$ sudo zfs list -t all
NAME                    USED    AVAIL   REFER   MOUNTPOINT
datapool                13.2G   2.41G   34.0K   /datapool
datapool/first          3.58G   6.84G   3.58G   /datapool/first
datapool/first
@2016-02-17-14:55       18.0K   -       32.0K   -
datapool/first
@2016-02-17-15:04       0       -       3.58G   -
datapool/five           50.0K   2.41G   32.0K   /datapool/five
datapool/five
@2016-02-17-14:55       18.0K   -       32.0K   -
datapool/fourth         50.0K   2.41G   32.0K   /datapool/fourth
datapool/fourth
@2016-02-17-14:55       18.0K   -       32.0K   -
datapool/second         50.0K   2.41G   32.0K   /datapool/second
datapool/second
@2016-02-17-14:55       18.0K   -       32.0K   -
datapool/third          50.0K   2.41G   32.0K   /datapool/third
datapool/third
@2016-02-17-14:55       18.0K   -       32.0K   -
datapool/vol01          5.16G   7.57G   16.0K   -
```

Okay. There are snapshots in play, so it might have taken some of the capacity, but still, why are the numbers different among the datasets? Let's first look at the _REFER_ column in the *zfs list* output. It states how much space the dataset is keeping references to. See that in the output:

```
datapool/first@2016-02-17-15:04        0      -   3.58G   -
```

The _USED_ column is zero, but _REFER_ is above 3.5 GB. That is typical of snapshots. Since the creation of the snapshot, no change was introduced to the file system datapool/first, so the snapshot does not use any space at the moment. But, it keeps references to 3.5 GB of data that datapool/first contained at the time of snapshotting. Let's make it use some space now by removing a piece of data I copied over to the datapool:

```
trochej@ubuntuzfs:~$ rm /datapool/first/Fedora-Live-
KDE-x86_64-23-10.iso
```

This gives us the following output:

```
trochej@ubuntuzfs:~$ sudo zfs list
```

NAME	USED	AVAIL	REFER	MOUNTPOINT
datapool	14.7G	930M	34.0K	/datapool
datapool/first	9.50G	4.91G	741M	/datapool/first

So, the file system datapool/first consumes 9.5 GB of space, but references 741 MB only? Where is the rest of the claimed space consumption? First, run zfs list -t all to see not only the file systems, but the snapshots also:

```
trochej@ubuntuzfs:~$ sudo zfs list -t all
```

NAME	USED	AVAIL	REFER	MOUNTPOINT
datapool	14.7G	930M	34.0K	/datapool
datapool/first	9.50G	4.91G	741M	/datapool/first
datapool/first@2016-02-17-14:55	18.0K	-	32.0K	-
datapool/first@2016-02-17-15:04	18.0K	-	3.58G	-
datapool/first@2016-02-17-15:22	1.20G	-	5.50G	-

```
datapool/first@2016-02-17-15:27  0            -  741M  -

trochej@ubuntuzfs:~$ ls -ahl /datapool/first/
total 741M
drwxr-xr-x 2 trochej trochej    3 Feb 17 15:25 .
drwxr-xr-x 7 trochej trochej    7 Feb 17 14:51 ..
-rw-r----- 1 trochej trochej 741M Feb 17 15:21 FreeBSD-11.
0-CURRENT-amd64-20151130-r291495-disc1.iso
```

Okay. So the file system holds 741 MB of data, but its snapshots consume 1.20 GB of space. That's more like it. Still, where's the rest of the space?

```
trochej@ubuntuzfs:~$ sudo zfs list -t all -o space
```

NAME	AVAIL	USED	USEDSNAP	USEDDS	USEDREFRESERV	USEDCHILD
datapool/first	4.91G	9.50G	4.78G	741M	4G	0
datapool/first@2016-02-17-14:55	-	18.0K	-	-	-	-
datapool/first@2016-02-17-15:04	-	18.0K	-	-	-	-
datapool/first@2016-02-17-15:22	-	1.20G	-	-	-	-

The output is cut out for brevity, but you can see that the datapool/first file system consumes 4.78 GB in snapshots. 4 GB is used by the refreservation property set on the file system, giving it 4 GB of free space at the cost of other file systems.

Make yourself familiar with -o space. It is going to save you lots of headache later on. While the almost empty non-snapshotted pool may not be very challenging, with passing time each added snapshot or reservation may add confusion. zfs list -o space is your friend then, but only if you befriend it yourself.

Index

© Damian Wojsław 2017
D. Wojsław, *Introducing ZFS on Linux*, https://doi.org/10.1007/978-1-4842-3306-1

Index

A, B

Access control list (ACLs)
    DAC (*see* Discretionary access
        control (DAC))
    execution, 78–79
    POSIX, 73
Adaptive Replacement Cache
    (ARC), *see* L2ARC device

C

CentOS, 45–46
CIFS, 84
Clones, 8, 71–72
Confidentiality, Integrity and
    Availability (CIA), 36, 38
Copy On Write (COW) file system
    deduplicated data block, 4
    graphical representation, 3
    rewritten data block, 3
    single data block, 3
    snapshotted data block, 4

D, E

Data security, 36–38
Dataset, 8

Discretionary access control (DAC)

accounts, 74
code, 74
data, 75
documents, 74
user/group, 76, 78

F, G

File system, 7

H

Hardware
    database, 38
    data security (*see* Data security)
    networking cards, 35, 39
    power unit, 33
    RAID controllers, 34
    RAM, 33
    SATA, 34
    SoHo storage, 31
    SSDs, 33
    storage, 29
    types of data, 31
    vendor and model, 32

© Damian Wojsław 2017
D. Wojsław, *Introducing ZFS on Linux*, https://doi.org/10.1007/978-1-4842-3306-1

Get the eBook for only $5!

Why limit yourself?

With most of our titles available in both PDF and ePUB format, you can access your content wherever and however you wish—on your PC, phone, tablet, or reader.

Since you've purchased this print book, we are happy to offer you the eBook for just $5.

To learn more, go to http://www.apress.com/companion or contact support@apress.com.

Apress®

Printed in the United States
By Bookmasters